T0193510

Thematic Expressions
for the
Lord's Supper

Comprehensive Practice of the Eucharist:
Themes of Scripture that Reflect God's Grace

Paul A. Hansen

WESTBOW
PRESS®
A DIVISION OF THOMAS NELSON
& ZONDERVAN

This book is a work of non-fiction. Unless otherwise noted, the author and the publisher make no explicit guarantees as to the accuracy of the information contained in this book and in some cases, names of people and places have been altered to protect their privacy.

WestBow Press books may be ordered through booksellers or by contacting:

WestBow Press
A Division of Thomas Nelson & Zondervan
1663 Liberty Drive
Bloomington, IN 47403
www.westbowpress.com
844-714-3454

Because of the dynamic nature of the Internet, any web addresses or links contained in this book may have changed since publication and may no longer be valid. The views expressed in this work are solely those of the author and do not necessarily reflect the views of the publisher, and the publisher hereby disclaims any responsibility for them.

Any people depicted in stock imagery provided by Getty Images are models, and such images are being used for illustrative purposes only. Certain stock imagery © Getty Images.

Scripture quotations are from the ESV® Bible (The Holy Bible, English Standard Version®), copyright © 2001 by Crossway, a publishing ministry of Good News Publishers. Used by permission. All rights reserved

ISBN: 978-1-6642-9574-2 (sc)
ISBN: 978-1-6642-9576-6 (hc)
ISBN: 978-1-6642-9575-9 (e)

Library of Congress Control Number: 2023905135

Print information available on the last page.

WestBow Press rev. date: 03/25/2023

Jesus Christ, the only Spiritual nourishment for our soul.
from
A Short Treatise on the Lord's Supper
John Calvin
For the Church of the Christ of God,
For the Glory of God

Contents

Preface

This book espouses a radical idea for the twenty-first century Protestant and Evangelical Church. Since the onset of a set, official, liturgy, the Holy Catholic Church, that is the Universal Church across time and geography, has followed a set pattern for its worship experiences. In many denominations, Catholic, Orthodox and Protestant have all codified these liturgies according to the respective theologies they follow. This book breaks into that tradition and heritage of the Church and proposes something new and different for one aspect of that liturgy, the Lords Supper.

While based on scripture, first, it also attempts to realign the liturgy to follow the practice of examination and preparation that is prominent in Paul's First letter to the Corinthians. This is part of the liturgical practice of Churches in the Reformed tradition. It borrows from the Roman Catholic confessional before taking the Mass.

I realize that this effort can appear to be dabbling into the set character of denomination or even a congregation's worship experience, as evidenced by Church history and nature of the Eucharist as attested to in the various strands of theologies of the Church. While challenging to church liturgical orthodoxy, I do believe that what I propose in the pages that follow, is very much in line with scripture and with Churches through history regardless of location. I also believe it is in line with what Jesus calls us to be, by being Spirit-filled and clothed, and to do, by following the call He gives in Matthew 5-8 in the sermon on the Mount, which is to say to be perfect as our heavenly Father is perfect Matthew 5:48 (**NASB**).

If this book sets your teeth on edge, ask yourself why? Is it because what it asks for is heretical, that is does it deviate from the Biblical norm? Jude 5-16 (ESV) *5 Now I want to remind you, although you once fully knew it, that Jesus, who saved a people out of the land of Egypt, afterward destroyed those who did not believe. ⁶ And the angels who did not stay within their own position of authority, but left their proper dwelling, he has kept in eternal chains under gloomy darkness until the judgment of the great day— ⁷ just as Sodom and Gomorrah and the surrounding cities, which likewise indulged in sexual immorality and pursued unnatural desire, serve as an example by undergoing a punishment of eternal fire.*

⁸ Yet in like manner these people also, relying on their dreams, defile the flesh, reject authority, and blaspheme the glorious ones. ⁹ But when the archangel Michael, contending with the devil, was disputing about the body of Moses, he did not presume to pronounce a blasphemous judgment, but said, "The Lord rebuke you." ¹⁰ But these people blaspheme all that they do not understand, and they are destroyed by all that they, like unreasoning animals, understand instinctively. ¹¹ Woe to them! For they walked in the way of Cain and abandoned themselves for the sake of gain to Balaam's error and perished in Korah's rebellion. ¹² These are hidden reefs[c] at your love feasts, as they feast with you without fear, shepherds feeding themselves; waterless clouds, swept along by winds; fruitless trees in late autumn, twice dead, uprooted; ¹³ wild waves of the sea, casting up the foam of their own shame; wandering stars, for whom the gloom of utter darkness has been reserved forever. ¹⁴ It was also about these that Enoch, the seventh from Adam, prophesied, saying, "Behold, the Lord comes with ten thousands of his holy ones, ¹⁵ to execute judgment on all and to convict all the ungodly of all their deeds of ungodliness that they have committed in such an ungodly way, and of all the harsh things that ungodly sinners have spoken against him." ¹⁶ These are grumblers, malcontents, following their own sinful desires; they are loud-mouthed boasters, showing favoritism to gain advantage.

Does it propose something that would detract from the call to be a disciple of Jesus Christ, (follow me) and make disciples that follow the Word of God, Jesus Christ? Matthew 28:17-20 **(ESV)** *¹⁷ And when they saw him they worshiped him, but some doubted. ¹⁸ And Jesus came and said to them, "All authority in heaven and on earth has been given to me. ¹⁹ Go therefore and make disciples of all nations, baptizing them in the name of the Father and of the Son and of the Holy Spirit, ²⁰ teaching them to observe all that I have commanded you. And behold, I am with you always, to the end of the age."*

Does it offend scripture of the Old and New Covenant, twisting it and bending it away from the revealed will and person of God? 2 Timothy

3:16-17 (ESV) *16 All Scripture is breathed out by God and profitable for teaching, for reproof, for correction, and for training in righteousness, 17 that the man of God may be complete, equipped for every good work.*

Does it distort the gospel to the extent that it calls people to a different means of salvation other than the call, and gift of Jesus on the cross for our salvation and sanctification? (Galatians 1:6-7 ESV) *6 I am astonished that you are so quickly deserting him who called you in the grace of Christ and are **turning to a different gospel**— 7 not that there is another one, but there are some who trouble you and **want to distort** the gospel of Christ.)?*

If your answer is no to all the above, then I would ask you to consider reading further, look carefully at your liturgy and worship you provide weekly and then what I believe and pray will transpire if we take seriously what the next pages propose. What follows does not add to the gospel. What follows does not pursue a different path to walk to know God and receive His grace.

After considerable research from 2002 through 2005, I could see based on what God did in scripture, the Church was missing out on the benefits that scripture describes regarding the Eucharist. Luke 24:13-35 was a case study in this search and the foundational text that reflects what follows. While the results of this encounter with Jesus that was experienced by these disciples in their encounter with Him after the resurrection, were plain and manifold, they were in line with other experiences that are outlined in scripture when people encounter the living God. Simply put, they drew these disciples closer to God, transformed them from fearful weak creatures to bold enthusiastic disciples. I wanted to experience those same consequences of the closeness of God in my own life.

The school I attended celebrated the Eucharist numerous times during the two weeks I was there twice a year. As I researched and read, prayed, and discussed this aspect of worship with my professors, I began to experience something akin to what is succinctly described in the road to Emmaus story in Luke 24. My eyes were opened I began to see Jesus more and more as God had given Him to the world to be. I felt a rekindled passion and excitement about both worship and life; in other words, my heart burned within me. I could not wait to get home after each trip and share these insights and experiences with the people God had given me to serve.

Then I realized that what had happened in me was possible to happen in the lives of all those God calls to Himself. The joy, excitement, passion, and enthusiasm that were mine were meant for all God's people. The story we must tell is made more vibrant and real by the retelling of it through sharing the experiences of others in scripture. This is what God did and this is what God wants to do through and for us today.

What pastor would not want more biblical depth for each of the people they are shepherd over? What pastor would not want more passion for the Kingdom and a relationship with God through His Son through the indwelling Holy Spirit? What pastor wouldn't want people committed to the message of the gospel? What pastor wouldn't want his people to go out of their way to tell others about the amazing things God has done for them and will do for all those who follow Jesus Christ? And all from participating in the one act that Jesus calls us to do whenever we gather together. Whenever you do this, do this in remembrance of me; 1 Corinthians 11:23-25 ESV *"23 For I received from the Lord what I also delivered to you, that the Lord Jesus on the night when he was betrayed took bread, 24 and when he had given thanks, he broke it, and said, "This is my body, which is for you. Do this in remembrance of me." 25 In the same way also he took the cup, after supper, saying, "This cup is the new covenant in my blood. Do this, as often as you drink it, in remembrance of me."* While the interpretation of this text in its' full meaning in God's Word, is perceived differently by scholars, what is beyond debate is the reality of what scripture says happens when we come to the table of the Lord.

So, before you let your tradition, or your heritage or your own preconceived ideas of the Lord's table hold you back from the full benefits of being in Christ and celebrating with thanksgiving the gift God has given to us, read further. If you remain unconvinced you have lost nothing and may have even had your curiosity piqued. If what you read appeals to you and the scripture calls you into this new practice, there are instructions given that will help you begin to implement this new way of celebrating the Eucharist in your own church.

God bless you as you read these next pages. God bless you as you grow closer to Him through the work of His Son as seen through the practice of the table. And God bless you and your church as you reap the full spiritual benefits God has in store for us.

Introduction

If the title made you curious and you opened the book to this point, I'm hoping to whet your appetite further for what follows. What is the Eucharist for you? What do you envisage happening as you serve or take the Lord's Supper? What does the scripture say about God feeding His people? What does scripture say about seeing God and being transformed in our inner being and life by Him?

For too many years, I served, participated in, and celebrated God's gift of the table in a ritualistic, religious or dutiful fashion. Or all three put together. It was something you did because Jesus had commanded it be done until He came again. It was something you did to remember. It was something you did, because the Church has done it since that Thursday night of Holy week, and we should still do it.

Then I entered the Reformed family of Churches, and they added a time of preparation the week before. This was novel to me. A little foresight and personal spiritual introspection, a period of examination, by each person coming to the table, was expected. Beyond personal confession before God there was someone else, I needed to encounter to seek reconciliation in relationship. That is good! The text which refers to this and is used for preparation, confession and examination, is found in First Corinthians 11:27:32 (ESV) *"27 Whoever, therefore, eats the bread or drinks the cup of the Lord in an unworthy manner will be guilty concerning the body and blood of the Lord. 28 Let a person examine himself, then, and so eat of the bread and drink of the cup. 29 For anyone who eats and drinks without discerning the body eats and drinks judgment on himself. 30 That is why many of you are weak and ill, and some have died. 31 But if we judged ourselves truly, we would not be judged. 32 But when we are judged by the Lord, we are disciplined so that we may not be condemned along with the world."*

If I've still got your attention let's look at that upon which the rest of the book hinges. Without getting into a long explanation at this point, I was struck by certain facts: that there was a worthy way of coming to the table and an unworthy way of coming to the table. The way to discern the difference was to take a good hard look at myself and what my relationship with God and His body was like at that moment. If I did not avail myself of this opportunity, there would be a consequence in the present moment.

First, what is worthy and what is unworthy? The Greek word used for unworthiness is anaxios. The word means careless. To go through the motions comes to mind. Apathy as to what one is doing or why one is doing it is a part of this unworthy concept. I should care and I should care passionately and deeply. There is more. To come to the table in an unworthy manner is to come incomplete. That is the point. All have sinned and fallen short of God's glory. I am incomplete in myself. That is why I'm there; I am incomplete, broken and damaged beyond repair through my own means. But it is more than that. Second, my preparation has been half-hearted and without full attention to God and the Word of His Works on our behalf and for me. Third and finally, is my presence at the table a fulfillment of my discipled walk with Jesus? Is the work that I have done in the period of preparation and examination, regardless of how long that period was or by whom it is led or by what that period of preparation was directed and guided, *good enough*?

To be worthy, is to come with an intentionality and a passion for the transformation that we have by the indwelling of Jesus Christ of which consuming the body and blood is emblematic. To be worthy is to come with a full-throated roar of praise and thanks (eucharisteo) for the work that God has done for me. To not just appreciate it but to yearn for it and ache for it. Finally, to come to the table should reflect an accurate picture of Jesus Christ, a mirror image by grace through faith. Intentionality, passion, and a purposeful reflection are all part of coming to the table.

This understanding of Eucharist points beyond the symbol to a transformation, a renewal, a re-creation. What God has made He is even now in the process of remaking by the body and blood of His Son and by the indwelling of His Spirit. In participation at the table something happens; our eyes are opened to the glory of God and to what being in Him, union with Him does for us, to us and in us.

Now, if I still have your attention, we should spend just a moment talking about the examination. This explains HOW we can come to the table in a worthy manner. The word examine in the Greek means that an object, in this instance the believer, is put to the test. Another explanation of it is that this examination is a critical examination. It has an eye toward what is not right, what is missing, what is insufficient. We need to ask the question, Am I to take "*a critical exam about what is in me?*" The answer is the relationship I have with God through His Son Jesus. In what way(s) is my relationship with God deficient, and therefore unworthy? Put more positively, what can my life look like when I am what I eat, when I am in Christ and He is in me?

The answer to those questions is in part found in Paul's writings. For the sake of brevity, I will share just a couple of them. Ephesians 1:3-14 (ESV) reflects in part what it means to be in Christ. Look at the number of times the word "in" (as in; in Christ, or in God) appears in the following text: "*³ Blessed be the God and Father of our Lord Jesus Christ, who has blessed us in Christ with every spiritual blessing in the heavenly places, ⁴ even as he chose us in him before the foundation of the world, that we should be holy and blameless before him. In love ⁵ he predestined us for adoption to himself as sons through Jesus Christ, according to the purpose of his will, ⁶ to the praise of his glorious grace, with which he has blessed us in the Beloved. ⁷ In him we have redemption through his blood, the forgiveness of our trespasses, according to the riches of his grace, ⁸ which he lavished upon us, in all wisdom and insight ⁹ making known to us the mystery of his will, according to his purpose, which he set forth in Christ ¹⁰ as a plan for the fullness of time, to unite all things in him, things in heaven and things on earth.*

¹¹ In him we have obtained an inheritance, having been predestined according to the purpose of him who works all things according to the counsel of his will, ¹² so that we who were the first to hope in Christ might be to the praise of his glory. ¹³ In him you also, when you heard the word of truth, the gospel of your salvation, and believed in him, were sealed with the promised Holy Spirit, ¹⁴ who is the guarantee of our inheritance until we acquire possession of it, to the praise of his glory."

As you look at this passage and all the "in's" present there, think about what it means to be in Christ and have Christ in you. Ponder the meaning of the Eucharist and all that it holds out to us not merely in terms of salvation and grace but in terms of a transformative event in our lives. Is this something that drives me? Is this something that I want and want more of in my life? What difference will it make in me when I am IN Christ and He is in me?

The second passage that came to mind, is Colossians 3:1-17 (ESV): *"If then you have been raised with Christ, seek the things that are above, where Christ is, seated at the right hand of God. ² Set your minds on things that are above, not on things that are on earth. ³ For you have died, and **your life is hidden with Christ in God**. ⁴ When Christ who is your[a] life appears, then you also will appear with him in glory.*

*⁵ **Put to death therefore what is earthly in you:**[sexual immorality, impurity, passion, evil desire, and covetousness, which is idolatry. ⁶ On account of these the wrath of God is coming. ⁷ In these you too once walked, when you were living in them. ⁸ But now you must **put them all away**: anger, wrath, malice, slander, and obscene talk from your mouth. ⁹ Do not lie to one another, seeing that you have put off the old self with its practices ¹⁰ and have **put on** the new self, which is **being renewed** in knowledge after the image of its creator. ¹¹ Here there is not Greek and Jew, circumcised and uncircumcised, barbarian, Scythian, slave,[c] free; but **Christ is all, and in all**.*

*¹² **Put on then**, as God's chosen ones, holy and beloved, compassionate hearts, kindness, humility, meekness, and patience, ¹³ bearing with one another and, if one has a complaint against another, forgiving each other; as the Lord has forgiven you, so you also must forgive. ¹⁴ And above all these **put on** love, which binds everything together in perfect harmony. ¹⁵ And let the peace of Christ rule in your hearts, to which indeed you were called in one body. And be thankful. ¹⁶ Let the word of Christ dwell in you richly, teaching and admonishing one another in all wisdom, singing psalms and hymns and spiritual songs, with thankfulness in your hearts to God. ¹⁷ And whatever you do, in word or deed, do everything in the name of the Lord Jesus, giving thanks to God the Father through him."*

If you're still with me in this discussion, it could be summarized as follows: To come to the table in a worthy fashion, one that is prepared enough not by their own works but by following God and His Word and in an intentional way, with a passion for a relationship with God through His Son Jesus Christ requires me to carefully and critically examine my own spiritual life in depth according to the Word of God. The dual criteria used for this examination is, am I indeed in Christ and is He in me and have I put on Christ and in so doing, put off the world around me.

The basic premise of this book is singular in its presence and dual in its presentation. As I perceive it, the Lord's Supper should be celebrated more frequently, (read, as often as you do this, gather to thank, and praise God; do this, celebrate the Lord's Supper, 1 Corinthians 11:26). Because of that more frequent gathering, there should be a deeper dive into the Word of God with each celebration. This would replace the more surface look at the mere institution rather than the entire context for God's gift of His Son and Table to us.

To support this premise, I offer three assumptions which I have made based on God's Word. First God always provides for His people. Beginning with Adam and his clothing, to an Ark for re-creation, from Abraham and Isaac and the ram to the gift of manna, quail, and water in the wilderness, from the gift of His only Son to the continuing gift of His Spirit, God provides for His people.

Second, God reveals Himself in many ways for His people to see and know Him and have a relationship with Him. From the voice of God to Abraham to the burning bush, from the pillar of cloud and fire, to the tablets emblazoned with God's revealed will for His people and a way for them to give God thanks in living, from circumcision to baptism and from the prophetic word of God to the revealed Word of God as John 1:1 describes Jesus, God has and continues to make His presence and will, known to His people. One of the greatest of these gifts is His table with all that it symbolizes and expresses.

Third, as a part of historical and liturgical theology, Word and sacrament have gone hand in hand. One reinforces the other. One reflects the other. This also reinforces and reflects the passage cited above from 1 Corinthians 11:26. "as often as you do this, (gather to celebrate and praise God as well as learn of Him and follow him with thankful hearts for His grace and favor), do this (celebrate the Lord's table) in remembrance of Jesus Christ. (Amplified translation, mine)

Now picture this investment in God and His Word by your congregation, being read and devoured regularly, not periodically. Think about your people being invested in God's Word daily in a pointed way that directs our thoughts to who God is making us to be through the work of His Son Jesus Christ on the cross which is reflected visibly for us in the bread and the wine. An illustration will prove helpful at this point. There is a product currently on the market that advertises that we do not get enough of the proper nutrients in our system to help us live the full life that we ought to have. We can't get the full amount of these nutrients, so we need to take this supplement. When we do our lives are changed, transformed if you will. We have the ability by taking these supplements to have the full life that we ought to live. The question that is asked is, who would not want this? So, let me ask all of you; if your life could be more today, could be richer, fuller, more loving, with an attitude and ability to do more than you ever dreamed possible, would you take it?

This book is about just that. The Eucharist is not merely an element of worship in which we participate occasionally. The Eucharist is not merely a reminder of a long-ago event. The Eucharist is not merely a spiritual exercise. The Eucharist is not a mere memorial or marking stone pointing to an old event. So, now, what would you like the Eucharist to be and do in your life? This book provides not only a rationale for a more frequent celebration of the table, but also provides how this celebration can be more transformative than it has been. Would you like your Church, your life, your community to experience the real presence of Jesus and be changed to be more like Christ of God?

Here is the Biblical story to which I referred earlier that provides the foundation for this study and should rekindle the light of the Spirit in us so that we might desire more of Him, be more passionate about Him and more intentional about our lives in Him every day. What follows is from Luke 24:13-35. *13 That very day two of them were going to a village named Emmaus, about seven miles from Jerusalem, 14 and they were talking with each other about all these things that had happened. 15 While they were talking and discussing together, Jesus himself drew near and went with them. 16 But their eyes were kept from recognizing him. 17 And he said to them, "What is this conversation that you are holding with each other as you walk?" And they stood still, looking sad. 18 Then one of them, named Cleopas, answered him, "Are you the only visitor to Jerusalem who does not know the things that have happened there in these days?" 19 And he said to them, "What things?" And they said to him, "Concerning Jesus of Nazareth, a man who was a prophet mighty in deed and word before God and all the people, 20 and how our chief priests and rulers delivered him up to be condemned to death, and crucified him.* ²¹ *But we had hoped that he was the one to redeem Israel. Yes, and besides all this, it is now the third day since these things happened.* ²² *Moreover, some women of our company amazed us. They were at the tomb early in the morning,* ²³ *and when they did not find his body, they came back saying that they had even seen a vision of angels, who said that he was alive.* ²⁴ *Some of those who were with us went to the tomb and found it just as the women had said, but him they did not see."* ²⁵ *And he said to them, "O foolish ones, and slow of heart to believe all that the prophets have spoken!* ²⁶ *Was it not necessary that the Christ should suffer these things and enter into his glory?"* ²⁷ *And beginning with Moses and all the Prophets, he interpreted to them in all the Scriptures the things concerning himself.*

²⁸ *So they drew near to the village to which they were going. He acted as if he were going farther,* ²⁹ *but they urged him strongly, saying, "Stay with us, for it is toward evening and the day is now far spent." So he went in to stay with them.* ³⁰ *When he was at table with them, he took the bread and blessed and broke it and gave it to them.* ³¹ *And their eyes were opened, and they recognized him. And he vanished from their sight.* ³² *They said to each other, "Did not our hearts burn within us while he talked to us on the road, while he opened to us the Scriptures?"* ³³ *And they rose that same hour and returned to Jerusalem. And they found the eleven and those who were with them gathered together,* ³⁴ *saying, "The Lord has risen indeed, and has appeared to Simon!"* ³⁵ *Then they told what had happened on the road, and how he was known to them in the breaking of the bread.*

This story from Luke 24:13-35 (ESV) gives us three results of being with Jesus at the meal. Our hearts will burn for God. There will be a more enthusiastic and intense desire to know Him and then share Him with others. Where is the downside for us and our Churches? Read on, learn it, and practice these things with your people and see what God is doing in your midst today!

Second, our eyes may be opened to see God in a new way as well as our Father and then through His work in us and with us in the Son, Jesus Christ. Seeing the world and my own life for what it really is drives me back to a closer relationship to the living God in whose image I have been created and recreated through the Son.

Third, there is a new boldness and conviction. I am now more able than before to face the challenges of today with Christ through the work of Christ in which I share. This equips, enables, and encourages me to live wholly for Christ, through Christ.

I

The Need for Thematic Communion: preparation and Worship

Why another book on communion? Why would you pick this book up and use it? How will this book help you to share the Lord's Supper with greater biblical depth and meaning?

Coming from the Reformed end of the spectrum theologically, one could think that communion is a mere formality, something we do occasionally to fulfill the command to "do this until He comes again." 1 Corinthians 11:26 This is, at its core, a memorial understanding of the Lord's Supper. We will talk more about that later. As Protestants, we would not want to get too "Catholic about this sacrament stuff", and have things taken literally. We would not want to be too Orthodox and have things get too mystical. We would not want to be too Evangelical and be mechanical about this meal. Reformed folks are pragmatic and deeply entrenched in the knowledge of what we do and how we do it, as well as why we do it. We know what we are doing. Don't we?

Let us begin with a brief background on the supper. What Calvin understood the meaning of the Lord's Supper to be, simply stated and paraphrased is, the Spirit of God is present in the supper. This was a contrast in his day with first, the Roman Catholic Church which saw the supper become the literal body and blood of Jesus, a renewal of the sacrifice. The difference with the other prominent Reformer of the day, Martin Luther, was that he could not let go of his Catholic background and for him, the triune God was in, under, by and with the bread and the cup. This comprehensive but amorphous and ambiguous understanding of the sacrament proved to be a divider between the Reformed and Lutheran wings of the Reformation. In that same Reformed vein, a bit later, Zwingli said that the Supper was in fact just a memorial. We did it to remember. There was no personal or spiritual efficacy to it. One merely remembered the sacrifice of Jesus.

Before you say to yourself (if you are not of the Reformed persuasion) this book is not for me and my ministry, think again. In all Christian Churches, they celebrate some form of communion in some fashion or other. The style, frequency, place in the service and the importance given it are different depending on tradition. What this book intends to do is help all those who serve in ministry to deepen and enrich their Eucharistic experience and their churches worship and liturgy through attending to a more regular celebration of the Lord's Table. We hope to equip and enable those who lead congregations to share a variety of different passages to keep the Lord's table from becoming mundane and taken for granted. We hope to equip congregations with a deeper look at God's revelation of Himself through the means of Grace and the Word of God. We hope to facilitate the transformation of the believer through a union with Christ in the body and Blood of Jesus.

First, the Lord's supper is not merely a suggestion or an element in worship. It is much more than that. In looking at John 6:22-65 (ESV) especially vs. 35 "Jesus said to them, "I am the bread of life; whoever comes to me shall not hunger, and whoever believes in me shall never thirst. ", we can see that this sign points back to a profound Old Covenant reality as seen in numerous other texts in the Old Testament. God has set us free from the specter of death and from the stain of sin. This is not hard to understand since Jesus Himself points back to Exodus and Moses. The blood of the lamb, John 1:29 (ESV)" The next day he saw Jesus coming toward him, and said, "Behold, the Lamb of God, who takes away the sin of the world!" and the daily feeding on the manna in the wilderness, John

6:32-33. "Jesus then said to them, "Truly, truly, I say to you, it was not Moses who gave you the bread from heaven, but my Father gives you the true bread from heaven. ³³ For the bread of God is he who comes down from heaven and gives life to the world", without which the people would perish are clear.

Second, the Lord's supper as seen from the above illustration is not a New Covenant or New Testament conception, nor a snapshot taken from the gospels but is a "whole counsel of God" conception. What I mean by that is, the covenant made with Abraham as testified to in Genesis 12:1-3,15:1-7,17:1-10 and 22:1-14 (ESV), specifically, points to God's greater plan of salvation for all of humanity which has been fulfilled in Jesus. With Abraham and Isaac, it was the sacrifice provided by God in the ram in Isaac's place. The sign of that fulfillment was consistent with what God did with Israel in Exodus with Passover; the lamb God provided and by the blood of that lamb the people who believed and had faith placed on the doorposts and were passed over, saved. We see this in His crucified body and shed blood, the lamb of God given for the sins and life of the world.

The people of God were reminded by God through the narrative of His works for them, several times in the Old Covenant. In 2 Chronicles 35:3-6,10-13 (ESV)³ *And he said to the Levites who taught all Israel and who were holy to the* Lord*, "Put the holy ark in the house that Solomon the son of David, king of Israel, built. You need not carry it on your shoulders. Now serve the* Lord *your God and his people Israel.* ⁴ *Prepare yourselves according to your fathers' houses by your divisions, as prescribed in the writing of David king of Israel and the document of Solomon his son.* ⁵ *And stand in the Holy Place according to the groupings of the fathers' houses of your brothers the lay people, and according to the division of the Levites by fathers' household.* ⁶ *And slaughter the Passover lamb, and consecrate yourselves, and prepare for your brothers, to do according to the word of the* Lord *by Moses."*¹⁰ *When the service had been prepared for, the priests stood in their place, and the Levites in their divisions according to the king's command.* ¹¹ *And they slaughtered the Passover lamb, and the priests threw the blood that they received from them while the Levites flayed the sacrifices.* ¹² *And they set aside the burnt offerings that they might distribute them according to the groupings of the fathers' houses of the lay people, to offer to the* Lord*, as it is written in the Book of Moses. And so they did with the bulls.* ¹³ *And they roasted the Passover lamb with fire* *according to the rule; and they boiled the holy offerings in pots, in cauldrons, and in pans, and carried them quickly to all the lay people. ¹⁶ So all the service of the LORD was prepared that day, to keep the Passover and to offer burnt offerings on the altar of the LORD, according to the command of King Josiah. ¹⁷ And the people of Israel who were present kept the Passover at that time, and the Feast of Unleavened Bread seven days. ¹⁸ No Passover like it had been kept in Israel since the days of Samuel the prophet. None of the kings of Israel had kept such a Passover as was kept by Josiah, and the priests and the Levites, and all Judah and Israel who were present, and the inhabitants of Jerusalem.",* the people are reminded of the Passover and the significance of it. In Ezra and Nehemiah there is yet another reminder, Ezra 6:19-22 (ESV) *¹⁹ On the fourteenth day of the first month, the returned exiles kept the Passover. ²⁰ For the priests and the Levites had purified themselves together; all of them were clean. So they slaughtered the Passover lamb for all the returned exiles, for their fellow priests, and for themselves. ²¹ It was eaten by the people of Israel who had returned from exile, and also by every one who had joined them and separated himself from the uncleanness of the peoples of the land to worship the LORD, the God of Israel. ²² And they kept the Feast of Unleavened Bread seven days with joy, for the LORD had made them joyful and had turned the heart of the king of Assyria to them, so that he aided them in the work of the house of God, the God of Israel."*

Passover as the sign of God's saving action is prominent in the Word and was to be prominent in the lives of God's people. Jesus points to this importance and then applies this to His own call from the Father for all humanity, John 13-15 especially 15:26:27 (NASB95) *²⁶ "But when the Helper comes, whom I will send to you from the Father, the Spirit of truth, who proceeds from the Father, he will bear witness about me. ²⁷ And you also will bear witness, because you have been with me from the beginning."* This call is a reminder of Genesis chapters 12,15, 17 and 22 cited earlier regarding Abraham and the forthcoming universality of the promise of God for every tribe and nation.

With this understanding of Passover and the Old Covenant, we can begin to reinject the work and Word of God into the celebration of God's work at the table of the Lord Jesus Christ. It is no longer merely theology and tradition but returns our understanding of this means of grace to be a WORD dominant celebration. The Word is prophetic, personal, powerful, and filled with the potentiality of God and for His people as God indwells them. This celebration of God's presence and power is found from the beginning with Abraham to God's victory celebration in Revelation.

Third, since the table given by God is for the people of God to be nourished by His providence and work, the wider scope of themes that are seen throughout the scriptures will inform, encourage, and invite people to dig more deeply into the richness of the grace that God gives for their spiritual nourishment and enrichment. In that way it is not a mere memorial but is the table and feast that John sees in Revelation where we dine with and on the Lord for all time.

Finally, and what leads back to the Reformed tradition is the necessity of and rich meaning of the Eucharist tradition in the Protestant Churches today. Contemporary American society and Church need to hear this now. In a culture where human beings are seen as becoming better, (Arminian tradition of memorialization) or where people are seen to not need any spiritual life, (the "none's" of today's religious culture) or where people are seen as getting better on their own (the psychologizing of American Culture), we need to more fully understand the Reformed background and tradition. This is what we alluded to in the first paragraph of this section.

Since we believe that humanity is in our nature, and subsequent behavior to be, totally depraved, we require constant maintenance, (transformation and sanctification only through the work of God's Spirit in us). The point generated by this understanding is God's provision of deliverance is not just salvation in some future sense to eternal life, but a deliverance in the moment with a purpose both personally and culturally. Israel was supposed to be not only God's people but a model to the nations of the power of God in His eternal presence to re-shape the human being to reflect that they were indeed made in the image of God.

Total depravity over against the more Pelagian/Arminian understanding of the nature of humanity as not being that bad, calls us to an awareness of our need for God. This is so much so that we are unable to come to God, follow God, be united with God, live by the grace of God except by being aware of His complete Sovereignty of God and our complete need for Him to initiate and complete that work in our lives. It is that which the Eucharist represents. The lamb provided to Abraham, the lamb provided to Moses, and the Lamb of God provided to humanity all point to our **NEED** for God to work on our behalf. We cannot do it ourselves.

For this purpose, our depravity, we are in constant need of self-examination. Does my life reflect an utter dependence on God and His grace? Do my actions reflect not only a willingness to submit to God's will but the behavior of actively pursuing God's will? And how is my relationship with God? Am I really committed to and enthusiastic about my relationship with God through Jesus Christ? Do I crave union with Jesus and the transformation that comes with the indwelling of His Spirit?

The process of union with Christ, which Paul points to, indicates that the Eucharist is not a ceremonial meal, which is merely a part of a worship experience, nor is it a memorial meal so that I might remember something that I might forget, but a meal that actually does something for me and in me. This is due in no way to any action on my part but is exclusively a result of God's grace and work on my behalf. The union with Christ we experience and possess through participation in the sign of a meal, is found in both Covenants. It is experienced in the old Covenant as the promise of God expressed or implied and experienced (witness Abraham Isaac and Jacob to whom Jesus refers) and in the new Covenant as Union with Christ.

Under the heading of the promise expressed or implied, please note the following texts: Genesis, 15:1 (note all the texts that reflect the covenant of God with Abram/Abraham Genesis 12,15,17,22); Deuteronomy 28:1-13 (who is with and in the people of the covenant?); 2 Chronicles 16:9 (through the people of Israel who is doing battle?); Ezra 8:22 (For those who are part of the family and seek relationship with God, God is with and in them); Job 36:7-12 (who has been with Job and near Job and in Job through this time of trial and difficulty?); Psalm 23:6 (an example of much of the Psalms that point to God's presence with His people); Proverbs 1:33 (like many of the rest of the Proverbs, here we see the one who listens to God dwells in safety); Isaiah 56:2-8 (God's dwelling is promised to those who walk with Him); Haggai 1:18 (God is with those who are called by His name and walk with Him). There are numerous other texts in the Old Covenant that should look at which all point to the work of God in covenant relationship with us; this is sufficient for our purposes here. The point is that God has in mind a union with and through Christ a re-union with His people.

The New covenant that Jeremiah prophesies and is worked out for us by God's work through His incarnate Son, is filled with references to God's in-ness; union with His people. John 6:51-57 (ESV) with reference to the Eucharistic elements' points to this union. John 15:1-26 (ESV) gives us an idea of what God means when the scriptures talk about union with Christ. Romans 8:1,10 (ESV*) "There is therefore now no condemnation for those who are in Christ Jesus.*", "¹⁰But if Christ is in you, although the body is dead because of sin, the Spirit is life because of righteousness.", reflects Paul's understanding of what this union looks like and what it acts like as well. First Corinthians 12: 12-27 (My translation) "¹²For even as the body is one and yet has many members, and all the members of the body, though they are many, are one body, so also is Christ. ¹³For [a]by one Spirit we were all baptized into one body, whether Jews or Greeks, whether slaves or free, and we were all made to drink of one Spirit.*

¹⁴For the body is not one member, but many. ¹⁵If the foot says, "Because I am not a hand, I am not a part of the body," it is not for this reason any the less a part of the body. ¹⁶And if the ear says, "Because I am not an eye, I am not a part of the body," it is not for this reason any the less a part of the body. ¹⁷If the whole body were an eye, where would the hearing be? If the whole were hearing, where would the sense of smell be? ¹⁸But now God has placed the members, each one of them, in the body, just as He desired. ¹⁹If they were all one member, where would the body be? ²⁰But now there are many members, but one body. ²¹And the eye cannot say to the hand, "I have no need of you"; or again the head to the feet, "I have no need of you." ²²On the contrary, it is much truer that the members of the body which seem to be weaker are necessary; ²³and those members of the body which we deem less honorable,ʲ on these we bestow more abundant honor, and our less presentable members become much more presentable, ²⁴whereas our more presentable members have no need of it. But God has so composed the body, giving more abundant honor to that member which lacked, ²⁵so that there may be no division in the body, but that the members may have the same care for one another. ²⁶And if one member suffers, all the members suffer with it; if one member is honored, all the members rejoice with it.

²⁷Now you are Christ's body, and individually members of it.", gives a visual image to this sense of being one with Christ and being joined to Him. All of this could be summarized by the passage in Colossians 1:27

(ESV), which says," ²⁷ *To them God chose to make known how great among the Gentiles are the riches of the glory of this mystery, which is Christ in you, the hope of glory."*

It is plain from this that the Lord's table, meaning the bread of life and the cup of His blood is more than the elements they are, the symbols they represent, and a way to remember Jesus and His work for us. As with the elements of blood of the lamb on the evening of Passover, they do something. As with the manna in the desert, it does something. We are missing out on the full benefits of the gift of God given to us in the body of His Son Jesus Christ.

In the Reformed tradition it has been and today more than ever a need for us as a covenant family to come to the table prepared. This is based on Paul's rejoinder to the Corinthian church to "examine themselves", 1 Corinthians 11:26 as they come to the table, so that they may not eat and drink damnation to themselves. What are they examining? Regarding depravity, their utter and complete need for God, with regard to sovereignty, their inability to provide for their own spiritual life, wellbeing and future development and with regard to union with Christ, if their lives truly were being sanctified, transformed to be like Christ.

All this preparation has a purpose. If or when we see the supper only as a memorial, we deprive that meal that God has given of the power and efficacy it is meant to have. The lamb for the sacrifice was given to Abraham or Israel or through the ministry of Moses as a substitute for something else, not a memorial symbol. For Abraham that lamb (ram) meant life for Isaac and a future for his family. God substituted the lamb (ram) for that which for which God required, Isaac. For Moses and Israel that lamb was not a part of dinner to be remembered as part of a future menu but was substituted for life that was required by God, therefore, life and freedom for Israel.

The bread was not given from Melchizedek to Abraham Genesis 14:17-24 (NASB95) as a mid-morning snack but was a sign of peace and recognition of who Abraham was in God's eyes. The manna was not only given to keep Israel alive which it was, but it was a reminder of how God would provide for them and for them to rely on Him for their future each day, Exodus 16:3-4, 14-15. *"³ and the people of Israel said to them, "Would that we had died by the hand of the* LORD *in the land of Egypt, when we sat by the meat pots and ate bread to the full, for you have brought us out into this wilderness to kill this whole assembly with hunger."*

⁴ Then the LORD said to Moses, "Behold, I am about to rain bread from heaven for you, and the people shall go out and gather a day's portion every day, that I may test them, whether they will walk in my law or not. ¹⁴ And when the dew had gone up, there was on the face of the wilderness a fine, flake-like thing, fine as frost on the ground. ¹⁵ When the people of Israel saw it, they said to one another, "What is it?" For they did not know what it was. And Moses said to them, "It is the bread that the LORD has given you to eat."

For us, the Lord's Supper is not a meal as a part of worship on a periodic basis, but it is a meal with a consequence in our lives. Something should happen. Something should change. It is God's gift to us and has been His gift to His people throughout revealed history. When we see what the whole counsel of God says regarding this feast, we begin to more fully understand and appreciate the breadth and depth of our communion with God through Jesus Christ and what can, and in a deeper spiritual way, is happening in our lives.

In addition, when we consider that for all Christians, whether understood as a goal or a consequence, we will live with Jesus's forever. For those of us who look forward to this lifestyle, we begin now. Whenever we meet with the body of Christ we participate in the feast of Christ. Psalm 23:5 points us toward it, when it says, "he prepares a table for us...." In the gospels Jesus confirms it when He says He won't drink of it again, until He comes in His kingdom Matthew 26:26-29, and Revelation points to the fulfillment of it when we sit down with Him as the bride of Jesus at the wedding feast, Revelation 21:2ff.

The celebration of this feast is both grace and judgment. While Jesus says in John 3:16-17 He did not come into the world to condemn the world but rather save the world through the love of God and by His grace, the passage also says that those who refuse to believe already stand condemned. Paul reaffirms this concept. We can by not believing in Jesus and putting on Christ as well as being in union with Him, eat and drink condemnation to ourselves. It is this principle of God's condemnation and judgment that needs to be folded into our thinking along with the sense of God's grace and hope through the work of His Son, that God gives. It is the opposing consequences that are present in the Supper. It is for the reason of judgment that we are challenged to prepare to come to the table and to examine ourselves as to how and in whom we are living our lives.

As with the Passover meal for Israel in Egypt, there is both salvation and condemnation, life, and death, blessing and curse. In a world that denies the reality of hell and judgment, or compromises and diminishes it, we are warned through the story of Passover, that what God has done through His Son's work on the cross and resurrection, is to be not only received but also taken in and made part of our lives. As with the exodus for Israel, so the life of Christ and the cross for the world today.

To receive Jesus as savior and believe in Him as Lord of our life is confirmed at the table. But there is a predicate to the reception. Do you believe? This is not an intellectual assent any more than in Egypt, the believing Jew would say "I believe what Moses said" but do nothing about it. There is blood on the doorpost. There would be the Passover meal eaten in haste and there would be the willingness to leave Egypt and follow God/ Moses leading.

As with the first Passover there is the preparation that takes place today as well. The Hebrews were to tell the story. The children were to seek out the leaven from the house to remove the stain of sin. The Passover meal would have then be eaten and the rehearsal of the story of God's intervention and work of salvation which would be lived out again at that moment for that family. For us today ought to be that sense of preparation as well.

Are we hearing the story of God's saving work through His Son on the cross? Do we know Him better and follow Him more closely? Are we receiving the benefits of the life of Jesus through the Spirit given? All this falls under the heading of preparation. This is so much more than a five-minute exercise the Sunday before we come to the table even if that five-minute exercise includes a prayer of confession. It is so much more than walking into the sanctuary on the day of the Lord's Supper and saying, "oh that is right… I need to get right with God."

So, here is the deal! Do we look forward to and anticipate that wonderful day when we will sit with Jesus EVERY day and dine with Him? For those for whom this is the desire of their heart, to praise God and enjoy Him forever as the Westminster Catechism states, they should be ecstatic when faced with the opportunity to feast with Jesus as often as possible. And if that is something we anticipate and look forward to, what better way to do that then to understand and experience the full range and depth of this relationship with Jesus Christ.

To know our sin better is to appreciate the sacrifice more. To know the full measure of the gift of God in His Son is to be able to be more grateful and live a life of thanksgiving before God, (guilt, grace, and gratitude as the three headings of the Heidelberg Catechism lay out). In our thanksgiving, a lifestyle that is lived that reflects God's presence, power, love, and care to the world around us.

II

The Deficit of Confession and Preparation, Filled

The core prerequisite of the Lord's Supper for the church before the reformation (Roman Catholic) and in the Reformed faith (Lutheran and Reformed Churches) is profession and confession. This is not just a Reformed construct. In the Roman Catholic Church, profession and confession before Mass is an absolute. While there is room for criticism of the Roman Catholic manner of coming to the table, it should be noted here that the Roman Churches practice presented here; to take time to ponder your sins and seek absolution for them, prior to coming to the Mass, is instructive for us.

While the understanding of what happens in the confessional as well as at the table is not the view of the protestant church and in particular the Reformed Church, it would be wise of us to consider not the fashion of the practice but the seriousness with which they approach the table. What the Roman Catholic Church does with a priest, we put in the hands of the individual. The individual congregant is challenged by the reinforcing of a relationship with God and the body, to come before God and pursue a right relationship with Him before coming to the table. The call to communion by the leadership, council, elders or pastor, the week prior is designed to prick the conscience of the Reformed believer.

The confessional becomes private rather than open to the Church. The question we must answer is, do we appropriate this opportunity or merely pay lip service to it?

In the Orthodox Church it is a part of the Eucharistic Liturgy. It was to be a spiritual cleansing a time of drawing nearer God which begins with confession, (See Isaiah 6:1-5 (**ESV**) *[4] And the foundations of the thresholds shook at the voice of him who called, and the house was filled with smoke. [5] And I said: "Woe is me! For I am lost; for I am a man of unclean lips, and I dwell in the midst of a people of unclean lips; for my eyes have seen the King, the LORD of hosts!"[6] Then one of the seraphim flew to me, having in his hand a burning coal that he had taken with tongs from the altar.*) What this text from the Old Testament echoes in the New Testament reflects regarding the celebration of the sign of God's work, is the awareness of sin, self-examination, and the forgiveness only God can give, in conjunction with the Word of God. This precedes the call of God to ministry and the presumes the need for constant grace giving through God's work.

Point of fact is that according to Rev. Thomas Fitzgerald of the Greek orthodox Church, "Prior to the beginning of the Liturgy, the priest prepares himself with prayer and then precedes to vest himself." "The vestments express his priestly ministry as well as his office." [1] "He then prepares the offering of bread and wine for the Liturgy."[2] Note that what is prepared is the bread and wine as well as the intermediary for the Eucharist, the priest.

In another part of this brief explanation about orthodox Eucharist Liturgy they say, "Everything in the Church leads to the Eucharist and all things flow from it." "…The Passover meal was transformed by Christ into an act done in remembrance of Him; of His life, death and resurrection as the new and eternal Passover Lamb who frees men from the slavery of evil, ignorance and death and transfers them into life of the Kingdom of God." [3] This meaning fits nicely with not only the ancient practices of both Israel and the Church but scripture as well, Luke 22:7-16 *(ESV) [7] Then came the day of Unleavened Bread, on which the Passover lamb had to be sacrificed. [8] So Jesus sent Peter and John, saying, "Go and prepare the Passover for us, that we may eat it." [9] They said to him, "Where will you have us prepare it?" [10] He*

---

[1]   Reverend Thomas Fitzgerald, Website of the Greek Orthodox Church.

[2]   Ibid.

[3]   OCA.org, Volume II, the Sacraments, Holy Communion.

said to them, "Behold, when you have entered the city, a man carrying a jar of water will meet you. Follow him into the house that he enters *11* and tell the master of the house, 'The Teacher says to you, Where is the guest room, where I may eat the Passover with my disciples?' *12* And he will show you a large upper room furnished; prepare it there." *13* And they went and found it just as he had told them, and they prepared Passover.

14 And when the hour came, he reclined at table, and the apostles with him. *15* And he said to them, "I have earnestly desired to eat this Passover with you before I suffer. *16* For I tell you I will not eat it[c] until it is fulfilled in the kingdom of God." And Hebrews 2:14-18 (ESV), *14* Since therefore the children share in flesh and blood, he himself likewise partook of the same things, that through death he might destroy the one who has the power of death, that is, the devil, *15* and deliver all those who through fear of death were subject to lifelong slavery. *16* For surely it is not angels that he helps, but he helps the offspring of Abraham. *17* Therefore he had to be made like his brothers in every respect, so that he might become a merciful and faithful high priest in the service of God, to make propitiation for the sins of the people. *18* For because he himself has suffered when tempted, he is able to help those who are being tempted. And then the writer of Hebrews continues in Hebrews 3:7-12, (ESV) "Today, if you hear his voice,

8 do not harden your hearts as in the rebellion,
on the day of testing in the wilderness,
9 where your fathers put me to the test
and saw my works for forty years.
10 Therefore I was provoked with that generation,
and said, 'They always go astray in their heart;
they have not known my ways.'
11 As I swore in my wrath,
'They shall not enter my rest.'"
12 Take care, brothers, lest there be in any of you an evil, unbelieving heart, leading you to fall away from the living God.

The article goes on in its explanation, that "(the word) Eucharist, is given to the sacred meal not only to the elements of bread and wine but to the whole act of gathering, praying, reading Holy Scripture, and proclaiming God's Word remembering Christ and eating and drinking His Body and Blood in communion with God the Father, by the Holy Spirit. The word

Eucharist is used because the all-embracing meaning of the Lord's banquet is that of thanksgiving to God in Christ and the Holy Spirit for all that He has done in making, saving, and glorifying the world."[4]

The upshot of the Liturgy of Eucharist is the union of the recipient with God through the sign and seal of Jesus Christ as evidenced through the Word and elements of the sacrament, the bread, and wine. In reading a substantial portion of both the theology and Liturgy of the Orthodox churches celebration of the Lord's Supper, there is no mention of preparation and examination for the individual believer. And that is the point of separation that I would like to emphasize. In Christendom, what we do in the Reformed Churches is unique. It is also significant and special for the Covenant family as a whole and the individual believer. The uniqueness is in taking time to prepare oneself through the guidance of the Word and Spirit.

In the Reformed Churches, the week before the Lord's Supper is served we have insisted on preparation which includes examination of the ourselves. This was to enable the believer to come to the table being aware of their need for examining their thoughts, words, actions, attitudes, and relationship both vertical and horizontal before dining with the Lord and on the Lord.

Examination and preparation are not merely, a verbal profession of Jesus as my own Lord and Savior and of that fact that I need Jesus and the blood that sets me free. It is an opportunity to get right on both the horizontal as well as the vertical dimension. As Jesus says to His followers, if you do not forgive, do not expect to be forgiven. In Matthew 6:14 Jesus says, *14 For if you forgive others their trespasses, your heavenly Father will also forgive you, 15 but if you do not forgive others their trespasses, neither will your Father forgive your trespasses".* If I have something against my brother, it is incumbent upon me to make that right or at least make the effort to make it right with each new invitation to come to the Lord's table. Can we imagine the consequence in the individual believer's life when they come to grips with their own sin(s) and the impact that has on all their relationships? Then there is the consequence of what happens to our witness to the world when we can reflect not only the humility and frailty of our humanity but also the depth and breadth of the grace of God in both forgiveness and salvation.

---

[4]   OCA. Org, Vol. II, pg. 2, The Sacraments, Holy Communion.

The all to brief announcement the week before," beloved in the Lord, it is our intention to celebrate the Lord's Supper next week," is insufficient to a task of that magnitude. Paul calls us to examine ourselves 1 Cor. 10:1-5,14-18;11:27-32 speak to this in this fashion: *"or I do not want you to be unaware, brothers, that our fathers were all under the cloud, and all passed through the sea, ² and all were baptized into Moses in the cloud and in the sea, ³ and all ate the same spiritual food, ⁴ and all drank the same spiritual drink. For they drank from the spiritual Rock that followed them, and the Rock was Christ. ⁵ Nevertheless, with most of them God was not pleased, for they were overthrown in the wilderness…. ¹⁴ Therefore, my beloved, flee from idolatry. ¹⁵ I speak as to sensible people; judge for yourselves what I say. ¹⁶ The cup of blessing that we bless, is it not a participation in the blood of Christ? The bread that we break, is it not a participation in the body of Christ? ¹⁷ Because there is one bread, we who are many are one body, for we all partake of the one bread. ¹⁸ Consider the people of Israel: are not those who eat the sacrifices participants in the altar? … But in the following instructions I do not commend you, because when you come together it is not for the better but for the worse. ¹⁸ For, in the first place, when you come together as a church, I hear that there are divisions among you. And I believe it in part,"* and then what follows is the formulary for the celebration of the supper, which finds at the end of it this challenge and warning, *"²⁷ Whoever, therefore, eats the bread or drinks the cup of the Lord in an unworthy manner will be guilty concerning the body and blood of the Lord. ²⁸ Let a person **examine himself,** then, and so eat of the bread and drink of the cup. ²⁹ For anyone who eats and drinks without discerning the body eats and drinks judgment on himself. ³⁰ That is why many of you are weak and ill, and some have died. ³¹ But if we judged ourselves truly, we would not be judged. ³² But when we are judged by the Lord, we are disciplined so that we may not be condemned along with the world."* I would commend to the reader to look carefully at the entirety of chapters 10 and 11 of Paul's first letter to the Corinthians.

There may or may not be a prayer of confession attached to this order for preparation. Then for the next seven days the intention in the liturgy and through examination and preparation is (hope?) that people will pause in their daily affairs and spend time considering the manner and substance of all their relationships.

I come from an interesting, if not unique, family that I am sure is representative of most if not all families. There is a division. There is rancor and discord. While it may or may not be on a monumental scale, it is prevalent, nonetheless. Now suppose we are all invited to another person's home and table, who is well respected by all of us, for dinner. We are not only having family difficulties but also are on the outs with the people we are going to be dining with that night. Imagine dining together with these people with whom you are at odds. Where there is no peace there is indigestion. If this non-peace breaks out into open warfare of words, there will not be dining in love and the expression of relationship in love. Now, also imagine that the host who invited all of us over in love, is in the necessity of his hosting, sit through this display of disunity and discord from the guests he has welcomed and for whom he has provided.

What kind of supper is this going to be? Between the nausea and indigestion caused by our emotions as well as the tearing of the actual fabric of relationships, there is the cold silence of people hostile toward each other and indifferent toward the Host who has provided the meal and invited them over. There will most likely be little gratitude toward the host for inviting us all over together and little gratitude for the meal. There will likely also be a less than positive response the next time the host invites you over. How do you avoid all these negative side effects?

There are two parts to this exercise prior to coming to the table. The first is preparation. What should happen under the heading of preparation? How does one prepare one's soul and what can be done to help people in that spiritual transformation and formation process?

Introspection is a prerequisite for preparation. For the Christian, coming to the Word of God in this endeavor is essential. This is where daily devotions come into play. This should not be in one book or in one Testament, but it should be the whole council of God. The reason for this is to guide a person through one of the numerous aspects of the grace of God that He has displayed for and to us. There are also activities or behaviors requested after each devotion that encourage a person to make a personal investment in their spiritual growth and formation.

The second aspect of preparation is confession. The devotions advocated for in this book, should lead each person to understand better their condition in sin and their desperate need for the grace of God that will be forthcoming at the table. We cannot appreciate the full depth and breadth of God's grace and then pray the prayer of thanksgiving with the full measure of joy and gratitude unless we fully appreciate our sin, depravity and truly lost state.

Confession is three dimensional and multi-sensory in its practice. The three dimensions are forgiveness with God, forgiveness of others and for others and forgiveness of ourselves. It is multi-sensory in that we need to come to grips with the things we hear, i.e., internet gossip and misstatements, what we see, intentionally, e.g. pornography, or what is taken in unintentionally, e.g. billboards and T.V. commercials or programs, what we hear, what we say, what we do both active and inactive and our attitudes or where our minds tend to go when we are not stayed on God.

We need to combine these two concepts and address them together. This is what God does with Jesus during those days of passion week. What the people did in their interactions with God, each other and within their own lives, (Peter, Judas, and Thomas as examples) we are challenged to look at and do as well. In other words, we must come to the cross and not as a singular event but as a journey. That is why a week of preparation and confession approximates that journey. What Judas realizes too late, what Thomas realizes in the resurrection and what Peter realizes and experiences of Jesus by the sea prior to Pentecost point us to the fuller meaning of the first Passover, (which also required a journey), and the second Passover, or the cross, and the journey of the week not just the way of the cross.

The more we appreciate and invest in examination and confession the more we will appreciate and be grateful for the work of God in our lives. It is for that reason that a period of time before the table is necessary. Since there is little symbolic in the supper, (Calvin says that the Spirit of Jesus is present and we need to expect something to happen), there is little that is symbolic about a 3–5-minute statement of preparation seven days before the meal.

It was related to me by a friend who appreciated worship, that the first time we approached the Lord's Table like this, (with a week of preparation), she was finally able to come into the sanctuary for worship that Lord's Day without the grimace of, "Oh that's right, we were having communion today!" What a blessing it is to prepare in advance for something that is not just deeply spiritual but profoundly transformational in our lives.

III

The Deficit of the Whole Counsel of God in Worship, Filled

One of the traits in the Reformed family of Churches I appreciate is the passion for scripture. And not just some of it. And not just occasionally. But the whole counsel of God, to the glory of God, in every aspect of the worship of God, for the kingdom of God, all ways, and in all circumstances. That being the case, one could argue that our worship services should be a full course meal sufficient to the task of building up the body of Christ and the individual members of it. However, and more specifically, our liturgies for the Lord's Supper, left on their own in worship, would leave a person starving amid a banquet table.

What I mean by this is, in too many of our worship experiences, we have substituted our words for God's Word. This is true throughout our worship time but especially during our celebration of the sacraments which is a part of the worship order in too many churches all too infrequently. Our calls to Worship are cultural pablum in too many cases. "God loves you and so do I," for example. Our invocations and greetings are too often our words. We seldom hear a prayer of confession with its attendant words of assurance from God's Word. As my mentor Dr. Robert Webber noted we have abandoned psalm singing in favor of praise chorus's that talk about our love for God not the greatness of the God we say we are worshiping. He called them romance songs or love songs to Jesus. Our prayers on behalf of the congregation are our own words when Martin Luther challenged us to pray the Word of God.

And then we come to our liturgies for the sacraments. While dotted with texts that establish the meaning of the sacrament, we tend to rely all too often on our own words to establish the meaning and purpose of the sacraments. We do have an alternative. Why not let God's Word speak for God's signs and wonders and the visible signs of His presence?

While we do base most of what we do in worship, on a biblical outline, what often fills our services are words and actions that mimic the world, not the Word of God. (This is emblematic of the community church, seeker driven/sensitive movement. There will not be a discussion of that worship style in this book). When it comes to the Lord's Supper, there are references to the Lord's Supper reflected through some of the New Testament, but these references are few and for the most part refer to the act of the Lord's Supper not the underlying signs of the presence and power of God on which and to which the supper points.

To do that we would need an examination of the gospels and the many passages that point to Passover or what we would call the Lord's Supper. For example, John 6:25-39 (ESV). *"²⁵ When they found him on the other side of the sea, they said to him, "Rabbi, when did you come here?" ²⁶ Jesus answered them, "Truly, truly, I say to you, you are seeking me, not because you saw signs, but because you ate your fill of the loaves. ²⁷ Do not work for the food that perishes, but for the food that endures to eternal life, which the Son of Man will give to you. For on him God the Father has set his seal." ²⁸ Then they said to him, "What must we do, to be doing the works of God?" ²⁹ Jesus answered them, "This is the work of God, that you believe in him whom he has sent." ³⁰ So they said to him, "Then what sign do you do, that we may see and believe you? What work do you perform? ³¹ Our fathers ate the manna in the wilderness; as it is written, 'He gave them bread from heaven to eat.'" ³² Jesus then said to them, "Truly, truly, I say to you, it was not Moses who gave you the bread from heaven, but my Father gives you the true bread from heaven. ³³ For the bread of God is he who comes down from heaven and gives life to the world." ³⁴ They said to him, "Sir, give us this bread always."*

³⁵ Jesus said to them, "I am the bread of life; whoever comes to me shall not hunger, and whoever believes in me shall never thirst. ³⁶ But I said to you that you have seen me and yet do not believe. ³⁷ All that the Father gives me will come to me, and whoever comes to me I will never cast out. ³⁸ For I have come down from heaven, not to do my own will but the will of him who sent me. ³⁹ And this is the will of him who sent me, that I should lose nothing of all that he has given me but raise it up on the last day. ⁴⁰ For this is the will of my Father, that everyone who looks on the Son and believes in him should have eternal life, and I will raise him up on the last day."

⁴¹ So the Jews grumbled about him, because he said, "I am the bread that came down from heaven." ⁴² They said, "Is not this Jesus, the son of Joseph, whose father and mother we know? How does he now say, 'I have come down from heaven'?" ⁴³ Jesus answered them, "Do not grumble among yourselves. ⁴⁴ No one can come to me unless the Father who sent me draws him. And I will raise him up on the last day. ⁴⁵ It is written in the Prophets, 'And they will all be taught by God.' Everyone who has heard and learned from the Father comes to me— ⁴⁶ not that anyone has seen the Father except he who is from God; he has seen the Father. ⁴⁷ Truly, truly, I say to you, whoever believes has eternal life. ⁴⁸ I am the bread of life. ⁴⁹ Your fathers ate the manna in the wilderness, and they died. ⁵⁰ This is the bread that comes down from heaven, so that one may eat of it and not die. ⁵¹ I am the living bread that came down from heaven. If anyone eats of this bread, he will live forever. And the bread that I will give for the life of the world is my flesh."

⁵² The Jews then disputed among themselves, saying, "How can this man give us his flesh to eat?" ⁵³ So Jesus said to them, "Truly, truly, I say to you, unless you eat the flesh of the Son of Man and drink his blood, you have no life in you. ⁵⁴ Whoever feeds on my flesh and drinks my blood has eternal life, and I will raise him up on the last day. ⁵⁵ For my flesh is true food, and my blood is true drink. ⁵⁶ Whoever feeds on my flesh and drinks my blood abides in me, and I in him. ⁵⁷ As the living Father sent me, and I live because of the Father, so whoever feeds on me, he also will live because of me. ⁵⁸ This is the bread that came down from heaven, not like the bread the fathers ate, and died. Whoever feeds on this bread will live forever." ⁵⁹ Jesus said these things in the synagogue, as he taught at Capernaum. This text points directly to the sign of the supper as a participation in the body of Christ, His life and Spirit.

While what Jesus says at this point is a direct reference to Passover which the Jews present should readily recognize, it is also a reminder to all of us exactly what God has done, is doing in that day, will do on the cross for all humanity and continues to do for us today. There are other connections from Passover to the Lord's Supper as well. From the bread (manna/body) to the cup (Cup of God's wrath or the cup that overflows), to the Wilderness wandering experience and being fed by God, (the action not just the element) and the bread and cup that were brought by Melchezidek from Salem to Abraham, there are multiple connections between God's revelation of Himself for the sake of His creation in the Old Covenant to the New Covenant.

What this book intends to do is give Pastor's and Elders an opportunity to begin to bring the whole counsel of the revelation of the saving knowledge of the sovereign God to the people of God, by leading God's people to an in-depth experience of the living God. Then we can equip God's people through not only the time of preparation but also through the liturgy of the supper in connection with the preached word, to gain a deeper understanding of and relationship with God.

There are a several parts in this process for us to apply to our congregation: frequency of celebration, variety of celebration and depth of celebration. Each of these parts will be analyzed and then dealt with, in turn. Assuming that the elders of the Church are supervising the sacrament, approval of that body and hopefully the encouragement of that body will go a long way in making this moment of worship meaningful long after the actual celebration of the sacrament.

The call of Jesus was to go and make disciples. This material will enable us to move past discipline to discipleship. I do not mean eradicating discipline but to at least move past it. Discipleship is to walk with another and lead them to follow Jesus. It is to learn at the foot of someone who has experienced a deeper relationship with Jesus. This material helps that process. Instead of simply moving straight to discipline, we can engage people to develop that relationship with Jesus that calls them into a lifestyle that reflects Jesus Christ to the world.

While the liturgy calls for examination and preparation in a cursory fashion, it can also point to a new path of growing in the breadth and depth of who Jesus is and wants to be in our lives. How much better for the Church, her witness, and for the people we care for if we could gently lead people back to Jesus and reveal more about the love and grace of God in their lives. What better way to be thankful, Eucharist, than to know better that for which you are thankful! Better reflecting God's grace and benefits points us to a more frequent not less frequent celebration.

So then, first, the frequency of celebration. Using the material of this book does not demand weekly or even bi-monthly celebration of the sacrament. Whether you are a weekly celebrant or quarterly celebrant, this material can help you bring the totality of God's revelation of salvation and hope to your congregation. The point of the Lord's Supper, which I pray will be made clear in the next section, is to enable people to see, experience and then live out through their lives and the life of the risen Christ in them. through the sacrament. The consequences of that experience will be clarified later.

Think about this. What shepherd would not want the flock to not just have enough food to make it through the week but instead have enough to be empowered to live completely through the week. Add on to that the joy of the salvation they have received. Add on to that the ability to express the gratitude to God who has given it to them through their worship and lifestyle through the week. The reality of the biblical meaning of the supper is union with Christ. As the bread and wine/juice become part of our body, so we are joining with the living Lord Jesus Christ. This union with Jesus has profound implications for the totality of what it means to be a human created in God's image.

As Jesus points out we love God with our whole body, soul, mind, and Spirit. In each of those aspects in union with Christ, we can see renewal and growth. How is this possible? Through the WORD of God in which we take part and dwell.

To do that, every time one intends to come to the table, they should and can open God's Word in new and varied ways through different themes, to give each person a new image of the sovereign God and His love for them. In this way, people can not only grow from faith celebration to celebration, but they can also be more impacted by the indwelling Spirit as they partake of the supper that Lord's Day.

The different themes then will enable the shepherd of the church to lead people deeper without the attendant complacency of "covering the same ground" week after week. This form of celebration of the Lord's supper forestalls the narrow, insufficient to the task, shallow image of the person and work of Jesus Christ that the living WORD of God present.

We can take advantage of the moment each day, to enrich the relationship through a new vision of the person of Jesus Christ each time we come to the table.

In the American Church currently, we participate in a unique "American Gospel"[5]. This gospel has taken several forms all of which deviate from the biblical gospel or good news that Passover points to in the Old Covenant and that Jesus presents through the presentation of the four gospel writers. First, we see an American emphasis on success. If we or when we believe in Jesus, life just gets better. What is most often meant by this is health and material possessions. The emphasis on the health and wealth "gospel" in the recent decades' points to a profound misunderstanding of God's Word. The sign of the Lord's Supper should and can be a reminder of this for us.

Another aspect of the American Gospel is how we feel about what we do at worship. Feelings are what determine action in our post-modern world. What I mean is, was I interested in what happened, did it make me feel good in general and about myself, did I enjoy what was transpired in worship, in the music or the presentation (read sermon). This form of worship was popularized in the 90's and persists to this day in churches of many different denominations. This particular style of working through the Lord's supper will be difficult in this style of Church. Over the span of time, it could be found to be more challenging and personally confrontational than enjoyable.

Finally, the concept of works. What used to be exclusively part of the Roman Catholic liturgical tradition, is now subtly added to many churches of different denominations in the evangelical protestant liturgical traditions. What I mean by works is anything the human does in a religious sense, added on to almost any church worship tradition that people do, which is expected to happen in them or to them, to enhance their experience of the living God. This tends to be most notable in Pentecostal style churches but is also found in community churches and other non-denominational churches as well. From speaking in tongues, to what was called the Toronto blessing, (holy laughter) certain behaviors or works are required to reflect the presence of God in a persons' life.

---

5   "The American Gospel", You Tube,

Regardless of the nature of the work, it is all a matter of what we do that reflects where we are in relation to God. This might well fall under the heading of the Golden Calf type of theology. It is what we do to add to and enhance our experience. Into that arena this form of celebration of the Supper enters. Here it is not so much what we do but a challenge to reflect on what God has done for us.

Variety is the spice of life they say. It is also a blessing to our spiritual growth and depth. In the sound bite generation in which we live, it is helpful to be able to supply a richness of an experience from many different angles.

In the world in which we live in the twenty-first century where Jesus is no longer foundational for many households and where the grasp of the extent of His work and the personal nature of it is vanishing, having the ability to see the glory of God from many different angles and perspectives even more important. Jesus is not one dimensional. Our worship and can and should be multi-dimensional reflecting the God we worship. It was in this fashion that Israel worshipped. Consider two examples. First of course, Passover. There were the obvious tangible events reflecting the power and presence of God, that the people of Israel experienced, such as the plagues that Israel experienced as well as the Egyptians, that struck Egypt over a period of time. Scripture records the screams that were heard by the Israelites as the angel of death passed over. The feeling of the texture of the foods prepared as well as the taste of them was present. Finally, there were the things that they were to do, especially the smearing of the blood on the doorposts.

The second example would be the Feast of Weeks or Harvest/Pentecost. Established after the entry into the promised land, it was one of the three obligatory festivals coming between Passover and tabernacles. This festival was 50 days after Passover and was a reminder that God's providence was in the harvest after He provided the blood for redemption setting His people free. There is with Pentecost the understanding of the bread of life which God provides to His people.

We can experience part of that today in our worship as we bring people to the table. As many scholars and pastors have seen when they have approached scripture, there ALWAYS seems to be something new about God and His work that is manifesting itself, in His world and for each of us. The newness and renewal of life finds as its source the Word of God. If we would have renewal and revival in the church today, we would find it in the bread of life, in the power of the blood, in the Word of God to which the Eucharist points and from which we receive the presence of God in Jesus Christ.

Variety also reflects that there is more than one song that can be sung by God's people. There is a richness of harmony in the song of the sovereign grace of God. For example, I grew up in the era where God was frequently perceived as wrathful judge. There was a bumper sticker prevalent back then with Christians that said, "Jesus is coming back soon, and boy is He angry." While I believe that scripture does point this out, there is so much more to God and His power and presence in the flesh on earth, Jesus Christ. *[14] And the Word became flesh and **dwelt** among us, and we have **seen his glory**, glory as of the only **Son from the Father**, full of grace and truth.* John 1:14 ESV (emphasis mine) It is this form of variety that we can reflect and develop as we use various themes of Passover/Eucharist on a regular basis.

The third consequence of thematic expression of communion is the depth of knowledge this can bring to the believer's life. In Jesus call and challenge to the disciples in Matthew 28, they are to make disciples. The word disciple from the Greek, maqhths, mathetes, from which we draw our word (mathe)matics, reflects that we are constantly in process of growing in knowledge. This knowledge of God is not an innate part of who we are, but we learn it and grow in it from others who have already travelled the path. From where do we learn about Jesus? The Word and Spirit.

Since the goal of the shepherd is to feed the flock, what better food than the body of Christ, the Word of God. This is done during worship through singing psalms, the prayers based on scripture, of course the sermon as well as through Bible Study, active devotions, and discipleship groups. The food we offer is the whole counsel of the Word of God. The food we supply is the breadth and depth of the revelation of who God is and how He manifests Himself to the individual believer and the body of His Son Jesus Christ, the Church.

In Colossians 1:10 and 2 Peter 1:8 (ESV)we can see this encouraged by the Apostles Paul and Peter. *Col. 1:[10] "so as to walk in a manner worthy of the Lord, fully pleasing to him: bearing fruit in every good work and increasing in the knowledge of God;" and 2 Peter 1:* [8]*"For if these qualities are yours and are increasing, they keep you from being ineffective or unfruitful in the knowledge of our Lord Jesus Christ."* I believe one of the reasons that the Church has conformed more to culture than Christ and has been anemic in its witness is our lack of understanding of how the Body of Christ (bread) and the shed Blood of Christ (the wine) can be more intimately be understood and appropriated by God's people through the sacrament of the Lord's Supper.

While this is not a book about the theology of the Lord's Supper, a brief comment will be made here. Why we ought to come to the table can have its' parallel impact in what happens when we do come to the table. St. Augustine laid a foundation for this theology and the Reformers, especially John Calvin, went back to it to regain the heart of worship but also the necessary ground for the growth of the believer.

Augustine asserted that to dine on Christ was to dine by faith. It was not as much physical exercise for the body. This is Spiritual exercise for the soul. This is for us in order to strengthen us for the task of living in God's Kingdom. As we embrace Christ by faith, so we grow in Christ in faith by dining on His WORD, Luke 24. (Sermon:) As much as the Passover was about the blood of the lamb for salvation, it was about remembering and taking part in the bondage of Egypt and the renewal of life that God would give.

To understand the Supper for us today, we need to begin to see things the way Calvin understood them when our current understanding of the Lord's Supper was in its infancy. Calvin opposed two separate ways of understanding the Lord's Supper. The first was the Roman Catholic way. The opposition was in two parts: first the substance of the bread and wine transformed into the body and blood of Jesus. Second, that each act of the Supper was a propitiatory sacrifice once again. Calvin and the other Reformers rejected both understandings of the Supper.

The second rejection was that offered by Zwingli. He argued that the passage that read, "This is my body," should be read, "this signifies my body". Zwingli claimed that the Lord's Supper is a symbolic memorial in which a person pledges that they are a Christian once again and that they have been reconciled to God through the sacrifice of Jesus body and blood.

Calvin followed Augustine in defining a sacrament as a visible sign of a sacred thing, or "a visible WORD of God." The sacraments were understood to be inseparably attached to the Word of God proclaimed and read in our worship experiences. Calvin's dispute with Luther and the Catholic Church was not over the presence of Christ, but over the mode or manner of that presence. Look at this difference this way; those who partake of the bread and wine in faith are also, by the power of the Holy Spirit, being nourished by the body and blood of Jesus Christ.

According to Calvin, the Lord's Supper is also a bond of love which envisioned us dining with the Father through the work of Jesus in a covenantal sense to bind us in love one to another. It was the body of Christ for the Body of Christ, the Church. It was to inspire thanksgiving and gratitude in the life of the believer. Here we see how it changes both worship, gratitude and evangelism, a life of thanks. The Lord's Supper, being the very heart of worship, Calvin felt that that it should be practiced whenever the Word of God is preached. Calvin considered the Supper to be a divine gift given by Jesus Himself to His people to nourish and strengthen their faith. As such, the Lord's Supper is not to be neglected in worship or in how we administer it but rather celebrated often and then with joy. [6]

Healthy food sustains the body. Since that food is indeed the living Lord Jesus Christ, John 1:1-5 (My translation) *"In the beginning was the Word, and the Word was with God, and the Word was God. ² He was in the beginning with God. ³ All things were made through him, and without him was not any thing made that was made. ⁴ In him was life, and the life was the light of men. ⁵ The light shines in the darkness, and the darkness has not overcome it."* This passage points to the greater reality that Jesus Himself brings up later in John. I and the Father are one, the purpose for why Jesus was sent into the world, who Jesus is to the disciples and who He can be to us, and finally to Thomas when he talks about faith and belief and how that is to be established for the believers to come who will not yet "have seen" Him.

I am certain that if the Church is to be as vital and dynamic in the twenty-first century as it was in the first decades after the cross and resurrection, we need to reclaim and reapply the understanding of just what the Lord's Supper is and how we can best experience it in our lives. More frequent celebration of the table with a broader expression of meaning through the Word of God will enable us to do just that.

---

6   Calvin's Doctrine of the Lord's Supper, Online article, Keith Mathison.

IV

Biblical Foundation for Regular Celebration of the Lord's Supper

Luke 24:13-49 is the biblical foundation for the practice of a regular celebration of the Lord's Supper. The story of the road to Emmaus supplies the ideal background for what we propose in the next several sections. The why of the Supper; what transpires in Luke 24 and the significance of the action of Jesus seen in the result of the disciples there, how the Lord's Supper's foundation in the narrative of God's actions seen in Passover as well as the preceding events of the ten plagues, is explained, what the Supper does, and even how the Supper can affect and change the person's life is provided in this text.

Beginning with verse 14, "*14 And they were talking with each other about **all these things** which had taken place*", (my translation) we see the necessity of the Supper on a regular basis. This verse can be lived out reflecting the power of God in the church by the Church today and every Sunday in which the Word is preached followed by the action of the breaking of the bread. The two disciples are talking about the things that are taking or had taken place that week but more than that how those events (things) related to their understanding of the Old Covenant. The Supper always happens in the context of the daily events of our lives. The world's events of the past week have had a profound impact on these two Israelites. Is it any different from any of us?

Verse 17, "*¹⁷ And He said to them, "What are these words that you are exchanging with one another as you are walking?" And they stood still, looking sad,*" (translation mine) provides the emotional background to this. What they have seen and been a part of for the past several days has left them bereft of hope and joy. They are lifeless. What had been expected from an Israelite point of view as well as their current Roman/Herodian context was incredibly disappointing and has caused grief at the loss. This grief is both religious heritage as well as cultural optimism. Again, in the world today, if you read the paper or listen to the news or check the internet, there is no hope, no future, and no purpose for life for much of our society. This has not changed from generation to generation.

The beauty of this passage is that Jesus is there during it. Calvin would say that the Spirit of God is present in the Supper. We see the precursor of that in this text. Jesus is present today for all of us though unrecognized even by those who think they know Him and His purpose, "*¹⁵ While they were talking and discussing, Jesus Himself approached and began traveling **with** them. ¹⁶ But their eyes were prevented from recognizing Him.*" *(Translation mine)* Here is the beginning of hope. The living and resurrected Jesus is present.

He inquires of these two disciples why they find themselves in the condition in which they find themselves. These disciples are spiritually empty, downcast, empty and without purpose. In our world today this is not how too many people, the faithful and those outside the body, find themselves. Caught up in the world, it is discouraging news and events, as well as our own preoccupation with how we are doing relative to others, we lose sight of Jesus and what He has done and would do for us. These two disciples merely do not see Jesus in their day-to-day life.

Jesus enters their lives at this point, (vs. 15-17, see above) and engages them in conversation. As we consider a Reformed understanding of Worship, we should remember we talk about Word and sacrament and how each supports the other as God enters the brokenness of our lives. Jesus meets them where they are; "what are you talking about," and why does this make them sad. Remembering that God is aware of our need, (the Passover celebration in Exodus), He engages with us and supports us.

Then a remarkable thing happens. This is where this guide to regular communion becomes more visible and necessary. After citing their lost engagement with culture and religious heritage and their sense of loss of purpose and direction, Jesus, vs. 25, "*²⁵ And He said to them, "O **foolish** men and **slow of heart** to believe in all that the prophets have spoken! ²⁶ Was it not necessary for the ⁽ᶠ⁾Christ to suffer these things and to enter into His glory?" ²⁷ Then beginning ⁽ᵍ⁾with Moses and ⁽ʰ⁾with all the prophets, He explained to them the things concerning Himself in all the Scriptures*", (Translation mine) says to them that they are foolish, (literally, this word is rather negative about the intellectual ability of the ones to whom this refers: they are unintelligent, and dull-witted). It can also mean that the disciples' personal desires or spiritual aspirations in this case were mistaken and misdirected. Consider how this applies to today.

In a world where people have: 1) chosen to ignore God or ignore what they know about Him, or 2) misrepresent God, or misunderstand God, or 3) simply turn their backs on Him, this passage speaks eloquently to the need for a return to regular Word and Sacrament. Paul speaks about this trait in the world in Romans 1:19-21 (ESV), "For *what can be known about God is plain to them, because God has shown it to them. ²⁰ For his invisible attributes, namely, his eternal power and divine nature, have been clearly perceived, ever since the creation of the world, in the things that have been made. So, they are without excuse. ²¹ For although they knew God, they did not honor him as God or give thanks to him, but they became futile in their thinking, and their foolish hearts were darkened.*"

The disciples in Luke have missed the message of God's redemptive work for the world (and them) and the consequence of it, the transformation of their lives by God's continuing to dwell with and **IN** us. They are foolish or dull-witted. The world today has missed the message of God and therefore the consequence of it. Nothing has changed. It is into those darkened hearts that Word and Sacrament enter.

This is precisely what the unrecognized Jesus does then and continues to do today. Verse 27 ff. points to the purpose of this volume. "Beginning with Moses and with all the prophets, He explained to them the things concerning Himself in all the scriptures." (ESV) As we consider why we should come to the table regularly and why it is also necessary to come to the table spiritually prepared regularly, the clue for preparation and examination is given in this passage. Go through all the scriptures and see how they reveal Jesus Christ, describe His call and will to us, and direct us in a Godly lifestyle that gives glory to God and empowers the believer.

Having heard the Word, the two disciples are engaged enough to request Jesus continuing presence with them. Whether it is expected middle eastern hospitality, or a curiosity about the depth of scriptural knowledge this Man has, they want His presence for the evening, *"²⁹ But they urged Him, saying, "Stay with us, for it is getting toward evening, and the day [i]is now nearly over." So, He went in to stay with them. ³⁰ When He had reclined at the table with them,* **He took the bread and blessed it, and breaking it, He began giving** *it to them",* (Translation Mine) It is at this point that the story takes a peculiar and unnatural twist.

The guest becomes the host. Instead of the two gentleman who had extended the invitation, hosting and serving the meal, the stranger/guest is now the host. Using ritual language used at the celebration of the last supper earlier, the guest takes hold of the bread and after blessing it, he breaks the bread in the same fashion as the last supper/Passover meal and gives it to them. He then vanishes from their sight.

Now something else happens. What happens next is the purpose of this book. The eyes of our two disciples are opened, *"³¹ Then their* **eyes were opened** *and they* **recognized** *Him; and He vanished from [j]their sight. ³² They said to one another, "[k]Were not our* **hearts burning** *within us while He was speaking to us on the road, while He was [l]explaining the Scriptures to us?" ³³ And* **they got up** *that very hour and* **returned** *to Jerusalem, and found gathered together the eleven and those who were with them, ³⁴ saying, "The Lord has really risen and has appeared to Simon." ³⁵ They began to relate [m]their experiences on the road and how He was recognized by them in the breaking of the bread."* (Translation mine) The text in vs. 31 says, "they recognized him". The reality of the meaning of the word is clearer than that. What happened at that point corrected what was missing in their first conversation as Jesus came up to be with them. Recall at that time, Jesus called them foolish or better, they were dull witted and unknowing. The promise of messianic promise of God has now been filled and fulfilled in the person of Jesus and the relationship he establishes with the two disciples. The meaning of the word recognized is to have knowledge of something, to know something or to know it through and through.

What caused this dramatic change? It was the breaking of the bread. In conjunction with the testimony of scripture, they have now experienced and therefore understand what has happened. Who Jesus is, is now clear to them. To what extent do we discount this story and cheapen it if it is true worth when we separate Word and Sacrament? For those who think they know Jesus and for those who need to hear the story and experience the reality of the power of the cross and empty tomb, we deprive them when we do one and not the other.

There is a consequence that the church is missing in all this as well. They go and tell people what they have experienced. They share the relationship restored with Jesus. This is something the church could do with more of today.

Outreach is not something to which we draw people, as in entertainment, but it is something we share with people, thanksgiving for what God has done as with the disciples on the road to Emmaus, that God uses to draw them to want to experience the same thing for themselves. Sally Morgenthaler in a 1990's book, "**Worship Evangelism**", sees an attractive worship experience as a draw to those outside the Church. There are numerous flaws with this concept. First, as Paul notes in Romans, there are not who seek after God. Second, the worship of God is not designed to be evangelistic, (though there is no doubt that it can be evangelistic!). Finally, as the Westminster Confession says in its first question and answer, as the first three of the ten commandments informs us, our worship is to be designed to glorify and praise God. It is a weekly thanksgiving service to the majesty and wonder that God has called and chosen us.

For those who have been wondering why we would consider a more regular celebration of the Lord's supper, your answer lies in this story. For those who are of the Reformed persuasion, this celebration requires a time of preparation as the apostle Paul challenges us to do in I Corinthians 10:17-32. The person is challenged, before coming to the table, to examine themselves considering Word of God and the life of Jesus we say indwells us and should radiate from us.

In saying that I would refer the reader back to chapters 2 and 3. Examination should not be a religious ritual but a deeper introspection into one's own life. To do that effectively we ought to be measuring our life by the Word of God. That presents the opportunity to do devotion and spend time in prayer and spiritual growth.

It also calls us to mimic the story of the road to Emmaus. Beginning with Moses and the prophets we should seek the power, depth, and clarity of the whole counsel of God. Like the gem on the cover, to see the majesty of God is not singular but a multi-faceted experience that brings us into the full radiance of what God's word reveals to us.

(See one of the FAQ at the end of the book. It deals in greater length with this chapters subject)

V

What does Eucharistic-inclusive worship look like During Special Weeks and Seasons?

One of the benefits of doing preparation for the number of days prior to the celebration of the supper is the added flexibility it gives for examination and preparation before coming to the table. Rather, than our call to God be narrowly defined by a brief verbal call to the table the week before and by a shotgun approach to liturgy that says much but builds little spiritually, with this new form there can be greater creativity and flexibility in our Eucharistic celebrations. The benefit of a week's long examination and preparation is clearly shown in this section on celebrations during the special days and seasons of the Church year.

ADVENT: For example, with Advent, there is the opportunity to serve the Lord's Supper through the "I Am's" of John. With five opportunities including Christmas day it might look like this: I am the good shepherd, I am the bread of life, I am the way the truth and the life culminating in I am the light. This is just one suggestion among the many that I would offer. The benefit of this is there is a natural flow, a crescendo experience, and an opportunity to disciple in worship using the Word and sacrament that provides vitality to the season as well as a return to the Spirit of Christmas.

With Advent being the season of anticipation there are other themes that may lend themselves to either a weekly celebration or one that begins the season in week one and ends with the Christmas day service. One could also add to that the end of the Christmas season that beings Epiphany. Any of these options bring believers and the congregation in a new way, into the life and hope of God that is given in His Son, Jesus.

Lent: During the season of Lent which emphasizes repentance and the giving up of worldly things to focus on our relationship with God through Jesus Christ and His work done for us, many different biblical themes could be used during those eight weeks. The theme of bread/manna with particular emphasis on the wilderness wanderings and God's providence can stand out. Following that the theme of thanksgiving would be one which could be done at the beginning to allow for leading up to sacrifice toward the end. That sacrifice could be general or with a more specific pointing to the sacrifice God has made of us in Jesus on the cross. The light of the world would be another that would fit nicely into Lent as candles are snuffed out (the opposite of Advent), pointing to the darkness of sin and the cry of Jesus on the cross of the abandonment of God. The total darkness of the day with the extinguishing of the light of the world can write its own devotions for the week. The heart of God and the high priest themes also lend themselves to this season. Lastly, to look at the "I Am's" of John would be a great theme to journey with through the season of Lent.

HOLY WEEK: The theology of this week can guide the direction of the celebration of the Lord's table. Since the meaning of the Lord's Supper derives not from the order of the week but from the essence of the work of God through His Son Jesus, that is symbolized in it, we can begin to be a bit more flexible with the timing of the serving of the Supper.

For example, if we celebrate the supper from a "Jewish" frame of reference, we might opt for a Thursday evening, Maundy Thursday celebration followed by a more solemn Good Friday service without the supper served. For that style one might use the Passover theme for the Lord's Supper. The power of this theme is found in following Jesus through the path of Holy Week from His perspective, that of a Jew of that day remembering and reliving the covenant experience of Israel. That would leave us with a lamb of God understanding which can point us to the saving nature of His sacrifice. The questions, "what does Passover do initially," and "what does Passover continue to mean," provide a broad and deep biblical and theological foundation from which to plan worship and lead God's people in the fashion of Moses, and then Jesus.

However, if you would prefer a more ecclesiastical/theological approach, there is a broad array of options for themes and celebrations of the Eucharist. The possibilities might look like this: a Palm Sunday celebration tied to themes of the "I Am's" of John. I am the way, I am the light, I am the good shepherd all lend themselves to a Palm Sunday celebration. Moving on to Thursday, the theme of the I Am's could continue with I am the lamb of God. Then on Good Friday the theme of either, I am the bread of life, or I am the vine, would tie in to the cross of Christ and what it means to be a part of the body of Christ. Holy week can be brought to a dramatic and powerful conclusion with a celebration of the New Covenant on Easter Sunday.

I realize this a considerable number of celebrations of the table in one week but consider the power and meaning of it if communicated well. Through the preparation time required to be done prior to Palm Sunday and through that week with a preparation each day for the days to follow, the entire narrative of Jesus walk through Holy week can be presented. The breadth and depth of the revelation of God's salvific purpose for His people, both Old Covenant and New Covenant can be expressed. Would I do this every year? Perhaps not as variety is the joy of God's creation, but I might do this periodically to inform and encourage the body to see the great measure of God's grace.

Pentecost: Pentecost is the season of new life, first fruits. As such there are several themes that might fit here that would enable the worship leader/pastor to reinforce their sermons/series. Themes centered around new life would be helpful. The point of drawing the Word together with the sacrament is to be mutually reinforcing. There may be other themes beyond the next chapter that would help an individual bring into sharper focus the work of God through the Word of God.

VI

Themes for Communion

Below you will find a list of themes for communion I have developed over the years. The reason for these themes to be included in this work is: 1) to whet your appetite for working through the Word on your own to find even more of what God has for us about His person, presence and will. In addition to those works of God, other themes are included, 2) to share with your elders and deacons so that they can get a better vision for how this can equip and enable their congregation for the work of ministry to which they are called. Beyond those reasons, they also,3) give you a leg up on seeing how these look and how the concept of devotions and use of these themes can be used for your own congregation.

This is not a comprehensive list. You may very well find and develop your own. (Instructions for doing this follow in the book) Following that you will find a few sample sets of devotions and liturgies that also use that theme.

- Passover (Maundy Thursday/Good Friday)
- Blood of Jesus (Good Friday)
- Redemption
- The Wedding Feast
- The Lamb of God (Good Friday/Holy Week)
- The Good Shepherd

- The Great commandment
- Peace that passes all understanding
- Bread of life
- The Messiah
- Light of the World (Advent)
- The New Covenant (Advent, Old/New Year's)
- Sacrifice
- The Atonement of Christ
- The Cup of God's Wrath (Good Friday)
- The Table was prepared for us.
- The Water of life
- God's Gift of Grace
- Behold I make all things new (Old Years/New Year's)
- Thanksgiving
- You're Welcome
- The Heart of God
- The Table of the Infants (Advent)
- Gratitude
- The body of Christ
- The Ebenezer
- Mediation/Mediator
- Israel/ New Israel of God
- Creation/New Creation
- High Priest
- Sabbath Rest
- All the "I Am's" of John (some of which I've listed here already) (Each of these should be done as a separate theme)
- General devotions on the theme of the Gray Psalter
- Themes on the five paragraphs of the order for the Lord's Supper in the United Reformed Church
- Remember
- Unite or Unity
- Fed by God
- Examination
- Parousia or looking for Jesus second coming.

Also included here are a series of devotions and studies for Pastors and councils to work through to prepare them to present and lead the congregation through as they begin to implement a more frequent, in depth and liturgically themed communion experience. Of course, these devotions are not the last word in what you may need for your own congregation. It is meant as a jumping off point and should be adapted not just adopted for your own Church.

VII

How to...

Lean into a more regular celebration of the Lord's Supper

A. Choosing a theme
B. Picking texts for the theme
C. Writing the devotions on the theme
D. Forming the structure of the liturgy
E. Writing a theme driven liturgy with prayers
F. Putting the theme into a service with Music
G. Driving home the message of the text through devotions and liturgy

A. Choosing a Theme

From ancient times the Church followed a peculiar calendar unlike any secular calendar. This Church calendar was developed to educate the people in the scriptures, to show the flow of God's story and to look at the whole counsel of God through the year. This was done on a three-year cycle and in some traditions following an "A," "B," "C," church year. By going through all three years of this lectionary, all the gospels and a significant amount of the rest of the New Testament as well as Psalms and Old Testament are read.

When choosing a theme for communion, the first question I answer is what season of the year are we in? The options for the seasons are: Advent, Christmas (more than a day but a season of weeks!), Epiphany or manifestation, (Usually featuring the three wise men), Lent, which leads to Palm Sunday, Good Friday, and Easter which is a season, Ascension day followed by Pentecost which is the longest of the seasons going all the way to Advent. Amid this there is an opportunity to celebrate new year's which might include the secular one (January First) but also the New Church year of education. Also, in our tradition we celebrate Reformation Day.

This is easy in picking themes with some of the seasons and times. For Holy Week, Easter, Passover (Maundy Thursday) and Good Friday, there are a number of themes that are proper though you can use those themes at other times of the Church year as well. The more often you celebrate the Lord's Supper the more frequently you can use various themes that might be suitable for that time or season by including different texts for the devotions and as a basis for the liturgy.

Themes can be chosen to reinforce the series of messages you are preaching. For example, during a series on Ruth, you could do a marriage theme, or a redemption theme. Both would be appropriate to reinforce the power of the Word of God as well as the consistency of that Word throughout scripture. In the gospel of John, using the "I Am's" would be a way of reflecting Word and sacrament.

Try seeing the theme of the Lord's supper in the same way that Luke did when he shared the story of the road to Emmaus, *"And beginning with Moses and all the prophets, Jesus opened the scriptures to them showing them all the things that pointed to **Him.**"* When we do that, we will be able to open the whole counsel of God, seeing God's mighty acts from the Old Covenant through the New Covenant in unique ways each time. By being timely and appropriate with each theme in its proper season or on it's appropriate day, we will be able to enable people to follow Jesus through the revelation of God's presence revealed in His Word, that He has provided to us through Patriarch, Prophet, and the Person of His Son Jesus Christ.

Using a wide variety of themes can direct the congregation to a broader view of Jesus beyond the light of the world during Advent and lamb of God in Lent or Good Friday. Choosing a theme allows the pastor/elder or worship leader, the flexibility of guiding a congregation over the course of year to see a wide array of aspects of God's revelation through His Son Jesus. As congregational leaders, we may be limited in our theme choice only by the limits of God's Word, which is eternal in time and the Spirit. Omnipresent, in its ever-present view.

There are of course some natural choices in theme as they relate to the different holy days and seasons. But it is wisdom to let the theme reflect the season to reinforce the message of God. With a bit of work, there can be the joining of the series a pastor is preaching with the season in which they find themselves married to the theme that they choose for serving the Supper.

B. Picking Texts for the Theme

The texts that are available for each theme are only bounded by your use of the entirety of the Word of God. Most of the themes outlined above will be found in the full scope of scripture, from Genesis to Revelation with numerous citations to each text. The most convenient way to approach this is through one or more of several different resources. I have used a chain reference Bible which can prove helpful if your topic is a biblical word, Light for example. Naves topical bible can be useful for other concepts and words like lamb for example. Then there are concordances, which supply a wealth of texts for different words, phrases, and concepts like mediator. Lastly, I have used more scholarly applications like the Theological Dictionary of the Old and New Testament to research texts for themes.

Regardless of what tool you choose to use, once you have researched a theme, you will find numerous texts for each. Store these up so that you can go back and use it again later without using the same texts for either the devotions or the liturgy. Each theme I have used over the past 15 years has enough texts to be comprehensive without being repetitive in numerous applications and for numerous celebrations of the supper.

I have found it most helpful to be able to follow the revealed will of God through the scriptures from Old Covenant to New. For example, if you choose the concept of covenant, one could look from the Covenant God made with Abraham using any of the references from Genesis 12,15,17, and 21 through God's revelation in the Book of Hebrews and the Revelation of John. There could be stop offs in between using Jeremiah and 1 Corinthians just to name a couple.

The word Covenant can be found in many scriptures as noted below. Choose the five to seven texts that all point in the same direction you are using for the theme that week. Below is a sample set of devotions for Covenant chosen from one resource of Faithlife Logos research library. The source is noted for you at the end of the list.

בְּרִית *bᵉrît* agreement, covenant, contract (280x)

Gen 6:18; 9:9, 11–13, 15–17; 15:18; 17:2, 4, 7, 9–11, 13–14, 19, 21; 21:27, 32; 26:28; 31:44; Exod 2:24; 6:4–5; 19:5; 23:32, 24:7–8; 31:16; 34:10, 12, 15, 27–28; Lev 2:13; 24:8; 26:9, 15, 25, 42, 44–45; Num 10:33; 14:44; 18:19; 25:12–13; Deut 4:13, 23, 31; 5:2–3; 7:2, 9, 12; 8:18; 9:9, 11, 15; 10:8; 17:2; 29:1, 9, 12, 14, 21, 25; 31:9, 16, 20, 25–26; 33:9; Josh 3:3, 6, 8, 11, 14, 17; 4:7, 9, 18; 6:6, 8; 7:11, 15; 8:33; 9:6–7, 11, 15–16; 23:16; 24:25; Judg 2:1, 20; 20:27; 1 Sam 4:3–5; 11:1; 18:3; 20:8; 23:18; 2 Sam 3:12–13, 21; 5:3; 15:24; 23:5; 1 Kings 3:15; 5:12; 6:19; 8:1, 6, 21, 23; 11:11; 15:19; 19:10, 14; 20:34; 2 Kings 11:4, 17; 13:23; 17:15, 35, 38; 18:12; 23:2–3, 21; 1 Chron 11:3; 15:25–26, 28–29; 16:6, 15, 17, 37; 17:1; 22:19; 28:2, 18; 2 Chron 5:2, 7; 6:11, 14; 13:5; 15:12; 16:3; 21:7; 23:1, 3, 16; 29:10; 34:30–32; Ezra 10:3; Neh 1:5; 9:8, 32; 13:29; Job 5:23; 31:1; 41:4; Ps 25:10, 14; 44:17; 50:5, 16; 55:20; 74:20; 78:10, 37; 89:3, 28, 34, 39; 103:18; 105:8, 10; 106:45; 111:5, 9; 132:12; Prov 2:17; Isa 24:5; 28:15, 18; 33:8; 42:6; 49:8; 54:10; 55:3; 56:4, 6; 59:21; 61:8; Jer 3:16; 11:2–3, 6, 8, 10; 14:21; 22:9; 31:31–33; 32:40; 33:20–21, 25; 34:8, 10, 13, 15, 18; 50:5; Ezek 16:8, 59–62; 17:13–16, 18–19; 20:37; 34:25; 37:26; 44:7; Dan 9:4, 27; 11:22, 28, 30, 32; Hos 2:18; 6:7; 8:1; 10:4; 12:1; Amos 1:9; Obad 7; Zech 9:11; 11:10; Mal 2:4–5, 8, 10, 14; 3:1

διαθήκη *diathēkē* covenant (31x)

Matt 26:28; Mark 14:24; Luke 1:72; 22:20; Acts 3:25; 7:8; Rom 9:4; 11:27; 1 Cor 11:25; 2 Cor 3:6, 14; Gal 3:15, 17; 4:24; Eph 2:12; Heb 7:22; 8:6, 8–10; 9:4, 15, 20; 10:16, 29; 12:24; 13:20; Rev 11:19 (copied from Logos 9, Faithlife publishing, Bellingham, Washington, 2021).

As you can see from the list above, there is more than enough biblical material to choose from on this and many of the other topics and themes that are listed here. This is the only resource in the library of Logos/ Faithlife. For some other themes, you may have a bit more difficulty and need to use more than one resource, i.e., cup of God's wrath. For the person who is assembling this material, you will find that you learn quite a bit about God's revelation of His Son Jesus Christ and what that can mean to His people.

You could return to the same theme, i.e., Covenant, and do devotions and liturgy with reference to numerous new texts. This is what I meant by broadening and deepening people's understanding of God and His revelation of His work and will. As you grow in depth and use these texts for the practice of preparation and Eucharist, so your people will grow.

Using this method for any of the themes given or one of your own discovery will yield a gold mine of texts to use for many different celebrations of the Lord's Supper before repetition steps in. By that time, you will have new insights and be able to write new devotions for each theme along with a new formulary for liturgy. As mentioned before, a chain reference bible or Nave's topical bible as well as other reference works can be helpful in researching topics and themes.

C. Writing the Devotions for the Week of Examination and Preparation

Remember the goal is to lead people into a contemplative look at their own life. This should embrace the vertical and horizontal dimensions. When writing Lord's supper devotions of preparation and examination, what we are aiming for is a guided tour through a particular aspect of God's revealed will that will promote 1) spiritual growth in our own lives 2) a desire to grow closer to and deeper in knowledge of who our God is, 3) a humble sense of shame and guilt in the awareness of our own sin as directed against God, others and ourselves (Psalm 51 style prayer and devotion), and finally 4) a deeper sense of our own relationship with Jesus Christ as the Son of God and our Savior.

To do that, we, as shepherds, will need to dig into the scriptures ourselves to challenge others to do the same. The task of digging deeper will be made more difficult by the age disparities we will face in our congregations. Frequently to reach the kids we dumb down the scriptures and devotions to a point where they no longer can accomplish what we intend as described in the four items above. Avoid this practice. Allow the Word of God to speak for itself through each set of devotions.

What I have tried to do to bridge this gap is provide at the end of each devotion an activity or a time to share a thought with the other people in the family. This of course can be done even if one is by oneself. The thought exercises developed in the devotions are designed to help people come to grips with the passage that has just been read but also to come to grips with how that passage and the Lord's Supper should change their own life.

Of course, the key activity and the one that would provide the most impact personally as well as congregationally would be for a person to come to grips with the consequences of their own sin. Take a moment and imagine what might happen if a person becomes aware of what they have done to others. Add to that a sense of how far they have strayed from their relationship with God. The moment of reconciliation begins with that awareness of how far we have fallen from our relationship with God. We then, in taking action personally, begin to move in the direction of being made right with God and begin to express the gratitude that goes along with that right relationship, and making things right with others and the joy of restored relationships. This may not be as easy as saying it here, but if approached from a biblical perspective, can begin a process of renewal, peace, and hope for others.

When that happens, we begin to see not just a horizontal reconciliation effected by the action of God and through the working of the Spirit in us that is present and active at the table, but the beginning of the vertical reconciliation that only the blood of Christ can effect. This happens when our communion devotions are used regularly to disciple people in that relationship of reconciliation and for more than the usual five minutes during a prayer of confession which may not even be done personally but part of a congregational prayer, which can produce a congregational and personal spiritual advantage to the entire congregation.

For this reason, devotion writing needs to be intentional, personal (that is for each congregation, not in a generic fashion of one size fits all), and comprehensive regarding scripture without being repetitive. This is easy if we are opening scripture, even scripture we have used before, when we see it with different eyes. When we see it in all its' breadth and depth, we can communicate that to the congregation.

So to repeat, when writing devotions; 1) pick a theme that fits the season and/or the series of messages you are preaching, 2) research this theme through the scriptures and avoiding your own canon within the canon (your favorite books or passages) using a resource tool that gives you the feel for that theme, 3) pick out the desired number of days you will need and apply the texts in the revelatory sequence that God has already prepared for you, (Genesis to Revelation), 4) write the devotions for each day remembering to focus on not only how this text reveals Jesus Christ and His work to our lives but also how this text speaks to our culture and our participation in it, 5) then write an application whether a prayer, an activity or a thought to meditate on.

Allow me to give you an example from one that is easy and prevalent throughout scripture: Blood. I use this as an example due to its usefulness, but also to show the ease with which this can be done for any theme. I am using only Nave's topical for this example.

The following scriptures are chosen out of the entirety of what Naves Topical Bible has provided: *Genesis 9:4; Matthew 27:4; Leviticus 17:11,14; Hebrews 9:22; Exodus 24:6-8; Exodus 12:7-23; Hebrews 11:28; Exodus 30:10; Exodus 29:20-21; Leviticus 16:14-19; Exodus 24:5-8; Zechariah 9:11; Matthew 26:28; Hebrews 9:18-19; 10:29;12:20; Hebrews 8:26-28; John 6:53-56; 19:34; Romans 3:24-25; Romans 5:9; 1 Corinthians 10:16; Ephesians 1:7;2:13,16; Colossians 1:14,29; 1 Peter 2:18-19; 1 John 1:7; 5:6,8; Revelation 1:5-6; 5:9; 7:14; 12:11.*

As you can see from the above where there are 30 different texts given, (and I was a bit selective and did not choose them all), one would be able to craft over 4 different sets of devotions from just this list and that is using seven days of devotions which might not be the case each time. This sort of exercise takes about a half hour or less. Once done, you have set yourself up with that theme for several more times.

When all that has been done, make sure to read it through for yourself. Did it work for you? Does it challenge and call you to repent and change? Does it reveal a new side of God's character that communicated something to you that was not obvious or at the least in the forefront of your mind as you reflected on God and His character? When we have developed the week of devotions along with the prayers and exercises that are included with them, we are ready to move on to the next step in the process.

D. Forming the structure of the companion liturgy for the devotional theme

This can be easy for pastors of Churches in denominations that may be liturgical (having their own orders for how to do the work of worship and with regard to the sacraments) but a bit more difficult for pastors of community churches or churches that do not have a fixed liturgy, (charismatic or more holiness churches). Having a structure to follow will enable the practitioner to be able to "fill-in-the-blanks" so to speak.

The first part of this process then is discerning what sort of structure you will use to bring the message of Jesus' sacrificial death and resurrection to God's people through the course of a service and the meal that you will be serving. If you are free to design your own, it would be wise to remember to include not only the historic elements of the Lord's Supper but all those that are essential theologically when preparing to serve the meal.

What I mean by that is; there is a reason for tradition without being traditional and there is a theological reason for every element of the Lord's Supper.

The first form of liturgy is of the Reformed persuasion. It is a form that includes Word and Sacrament. It follows like this:

- The opening (call to celebrate, greeting and blessing of God and opening prayer along with Hymn(s)
- Confession and Assurance followed by a response from the people.
- Time of the dedication of the congregation followed by a hymn.
- **Proclamation of the Word** (scripture, creed or confessional statement, sermon, and prayers (and a hymn)
- Congregational prayer and offertory
- **The Lord's Supper** (preparatory exhortation, The thanksgiving, the institution, the instruction, Prayer of consecration, preparation of the elements, invitation, dedication, service of the supper, Prayer of thanksgiving (Psalm 103)
- Hymn of application
- Sending and parting blessing

This complete form of worship for the whole service might be replaced and substituted with the form for worship below which includes only those elements surrounding the supper for which the liturgy is written.

If your congregation is not of a Reformed persuasion or of a different denomination like Lutheran, and especially community or charismatic type church, it should be noted that whatever Spiritual group you belong to, you follow what would be called liturgy each week for Worship. From non-denominational community churches and their flow from worship songs to hearing the Word to a closing of an additional set of worship songs to the more structured liturgies of Episcopal or Lutheran churches, we all follow a form.

The Four-Fold form of Worship described by Robert Webber which flows like this: Entrance, Word, Thanksgiving, and Dismissal, gives a biblical flow to worship. Under each heading will include prayers, responsive readings, hymns, and actions (Baptism, Lord's Supper) and so on. Each of these sections provides for the flow of the service while the content of each section may vary from week to week. The point is this: that every worship service has a liturgy and within each liturgy there is a place for the time of confession (preparation) and giving thanks to God (Eucharist).

The simpler form for the Lord's Supper as part of the worship experience begins with a preparatory examination. Now, if you have done the devotions during the past week and used that theme in the service the week before as part of the Prayer of Confession and Words of Assurance, you may make this more of a brief mention at this point of the service.

The time of confession or preparation followed by *formulary includes the instruction for the Supper*. As Paul lays out in 1 Corinthians 11, he says that what has been passed down to him (Paul), he now passes down to the church. The events of the week of Jesus' passion are recorded in this narrative. As a good pharisee, Paul points back to Passover as the precedent for this Supper. All of this should remind us of the frequent "pointing back" or the shadowing that goes on through God's revelation. That supplies the foundation for our instruction regardless of theme. In writing this part of the liturgy, use the texts that you have already used for the devotions. Explain them briefly in the context of the verse and show the progressive unfolding of the plan of God through the revelation of His Word.

After the formulary or instruction, offer a prayer in thanks to God for the feast that is prepared for us along with the Lord's Prayer.

Now comes the preparation of the table along with the breaking of the bread and the pouring out of the cup.

As each of the elements, the bread and then the cup is distributed in turn, the person serving as celebrant will say, take, drink, remember and believe.

The distribution of the elements is followed by a prayer of thanksgiving (Psalm 103 or another form for giving thanks like a hymn or another psalm).

Interspersed throughout this form of liturgy hymns and spiritual songs can be sung that reinforce the theme. More on this later.

In other traditions, like the Lutheran tradition, entire forms for worship with each individual detail provided, are laid out as well. The themes for devotion and liturgy are more difficult to integrate into those structures.

As mentioned before, Robert Webber has a fourfold style of liturgy that incorporates the ancient and contemporary in both style and substance. The Lord's Supper fits neatly into this style of Worship. The four headings for worship are: entrance, Word, Thanksgiving and Dismissal. You can see the simplicity of it. Within each of those sections you place the particular worship element that will enable God's people to draw near to Him, be in a relationship with Him, (talk to and listen to Him), be fed by Him, and sent out into the world for ministry by Him only to be engaged again the next week and refreshed again for the task.

The point of this whole section is to interweave not only the Biblical passages used during the week for devotions into the service, but prayers, songs, and the remainder of the liturgy as well. When each part of the liturgy reinforces the whole the central idea of the theme, (ex. blood for instance) is driven home deeper and deeper. By varying the themes, you can then broaden understanding as well as deepen faith.

E. Writing a Theme with Prayers

So often neglected or perceived as an afterthought, (not by you but way too often by me and too many others, in the past!), prayer in this form of liturgy is the solid foundation on which the structure of the Word and sacrament find shape and dimension. Prayer undergirds everything! There are several ways prayers should be added that will enhance and support the theme of communion. My personal favorite is using the psalms but also other scripture, prayers that are in collections in various works over the ages, and free form that we develop on our own for the theme of that week.

For example, praying the psalms using the theme of blood that we have used up above would supply us these texts: for example," Psalm 9:11-13 (ESV)

*¹¹ Sing praises to the L*ORD*, who sits enthroned in Zion!*
Tell among the peoples his deeds!
¹² For he who avenges blood is mindful of them;
he does not forget the cry of the afflicted.
*¹³ Be gracious to me, O L*ORD*!*
See my affliction from those who hate me,
O you who lift me up from the gates of death,
¹⁴ that I may recount all your praises,
that in the gates of the daughter of Zion
I may rejoice in your salvation.

16, 30, 50, 58, 68, 72, 78, 79, 105, 106. Other biblical texts I would use might be for example: Lamentations 4:13-14 (ESV)

¹³ This was for the sins of her prophets
and the iniquities of her priests,
who shed in the midst of her
the blood of the righteous.
¹⁴ They wandered, blind, through the streets;
they were so defiled with blood
that no one was able to touch
their garments.

John 6:54-56 (ESV) *⁵⁴ Whoever feeds on my flesh and drinks my blood has eternal life, and I will raise him up on the last day. ⁵⁵ For my flesh is true food, and my blood is true drink. ⁵⁶ Whoever feeds on my flesh and drinks my blood abides in me, and I in him"*, and others.

Praying scripture also enables us to bring the people once again into a deeper understanding of the Word of God. There are numerous great resources that I would use for praying using the theme picked for the Lord's Supper that day. Of the several that I have used, (and I will include these in the bibliography under prayer resources with their complete information), Prayers of Walter Brueggemann, Reformed Prayers for Christian Worship, A Book of Reformed Prayers, When We Gather, A Book of Prayers for Worship, Leading in Prayer: A workbook for Worship, Talking to the Trinity: Praying Publicly and Privately. Each of these is well indexed and supply a wide array of prayers for thematic expression of Communion and for regular Lord's days.

Finally, I would encourage the pastor or worship leader to write their own prayers that are tailored to not only the day but the congregation and their concerns at that point in time. Of course, that assumes a certain giftedness not only with prayer but also with worship and writing. However, the upside of this is that a person can bring to bear in prayer the specific character and needs of their own congregation. There is a book by Carol Slager in the bibliography that one should resource for writing prayers and praying them publicly.

The overall point of this section is to drive home the significance and power of prayer. This is not only as a way God has given us to communicate with Him but also a way for us to open God's Word and bring the saving knowledge of the mighty acts of God to our people. See prayer as not just an element of worship but as a powerful tool to shape a discipled character in people.

F. Putting the Theme into a Service with Music

For many people, the power of music engages them more deeply in their relationship with God. The emotional pull of music can carry a person deeper into the message of scripture through the words of the song. This is true regardless of the style of music. A good example is seen with Handel's Hallelujah chorus but equally as well with It is the hymn, It is Well with My Soul or There is a Redeemer. There are several new Hymn writers like Keith and Krysten Getty that we can be aware of as we look to engage music with the now forming liturgy for the Supper.

The real question is how you craft an experience in worship that will bring people into the presence of God to see Him more clearly and feel

His grace, love, and power in that moment. The goal is to not only to lead people to enjoy ones' worship experience, but also enable them to dig deeper into the character and person of the God they are challenged to worship. Music is not just an element but is frankly a vehicle that will enable you to carry the message of that theme via another medium.

Again, using the theme of "blood," let's take a look at just a couple of standard hymnbooks. (The Celebration Hymnbook which has gained widespread usage through a variety of denominations and the New Trinity Psalter Hymnbook which is being used in a variety of Reformed denominations are two used here. Other hymnbooks and sources of music have been included in the Bibliography section). There are fourteen different songs in the Trinity Psalter, that explicitly have the word or theology of blood included in those hymns. Just a couple for example. "Bread of the World in Mercy Broken," "Come Ye Sinners, Poor and Wretched" are just a couple from this section. There are eight hymns in the Celebration hymnal. This does not include other songs from either hymnbook that include the concept of or theology of blood.

At this point, the number of hymns and placement of hymns in the service become critically important. Again, the idea in the example of blood, is to reinforce the theme of the power of the blood of Christ in the atonement that God has given. From the opening hymn that brings us into worship, through the hymns around confession, to the closing hymn, each should be selected carefully to take people on a journey through the service to the throne of God via the cross of Christ. (Just a little sidenote: more research can be done by studying Dr. Robert Webber's grasp of worship; for example, "Blended Worship" and "Planning Blended Worship". In the Four-Fold understanding of worship there is an ebb and flow, a crescendo and a quietness that moves throughout the service. As one constructs this service, they should be keenly aware of that flow and bring people to the heights of God's glory as well as the depths of their own despair and then the grief and forsakenness of Jesus on the cross.).

Let me make a note here that the hymnbooks I've referenced are only a brief list of music resources that are available today. I mentioned earlier about Keith and Krysten Getty. There is a website called Hymnary.org, among others that provides resources for music, for the pastor or worship writer. By merely writing the theme name and letting the site do the work you can find numerous songs and hymns on almost any theme. You may have access to other sites or resources as well.

The goal however, regardless of tradition or style of worship is still the same. How will we lead people into the presence of God? How will we equip them to praise the God of their salvation? What can we as a congregation sing, both in terms of tune and words that will give glory to God? What more can we help them know and understand about the character and person of their creator and redeemer? These are still the key questions.

G. Driving Home, the Message of the Theme

Now go back to pages 40-41. There is that partial list of themes through which you can not only see communion but the breadth and depth of the person of God through Jesus Christ and His providence for us in Calling, Redemption and Presence. In Western literature, especially academic writing, there is the concept of the "golden thread." This thread is what not only holds the whole work together, but also can wind throughout that work. This is what we want to do with thematic expression of the Lord's Supper.

Since we have been using the theme of "the blood", what we will want to do as we go through this particular service which includes the Lord's Supper, a thread that when "pulled" will always bring us back to the central idea we want, which is the atoning work of Jesus Christ by the sacrifice of blood. From the opening call to Worship through our praise of God through hymns and prayer and into our confession, it is the narrative of the sacrifice of Christ that is seen. From the congregational prayer through the Word of God read and preached, it is about what God has done for us through the blood of His Son. As we come to the table we should see Isaac on the altar, and the blood sprinkled on the people, as we come to the cross and see the blood of Christ poured out for us. Finally, we should see the lamb of God covered in blood, that now stands victorious before the throne of God in Revelation of John.

Our Worship in just this one theme with just six or seven texts for devotions and as foundation for the service, can bring new light to people in the congregation regarding the person and work of Jesus Christ, much like the eyes of the disciples on the road to Emmaus were opened. It can be that way with each theme and with each celebration of the supper with adequate preparation and then execution by the worship leader or team.

So how do we get to this point? What needs to happen with leadership? How do we prepare the congregation? The next step in your journey follows.

VIII

A Suggestion on How to Lead Your Leaders into a More Frequent and Discipled Lord's Supper Celebration

One of the issues that will surround this departure from the norm of communion that your congregation may be currently pursuing is the lack of support, encouragement, and/or understanding of the leadership of the church. Below you will find one of the tools that I used in my Churches, to guide your leadership and then your congregation on the path of a more frequent, more spiritually contemplative, more introspective, and more discipled journey.

When shown how this benefits the individuals in the congregation as well as the congregation, leadership will move toward acceptance of a more frequent and more biblical communion. They will see it not as an element of worship but as essential not only to worship but to the spiritual growth of the people they shepherd.

You may not be able to gain acceptance for a weekly celebration of the Lord's Supper, but you may very well begin with the devotions and liturgy usage in your current celebration schedule. What Jesus says in Luke 24. As eyes are more open to the grace that God shows and the growth they experience in your congregation, you will gain acceptance for the more frequent celebration of the Lord's Supper along with the preparation and examination that go with it.

The series of studies shown below I used to facilitate the spiritual journey of the council of leaders. I hope that it will be helpful to you as well. I would encourage you to add to it or take from it but at least adapt it to your own congregation for use. Used in conjunction with a preaching series on the sacraments in general, worship and its elements, the Lord's Supper as instituted and used in the first century church of the New Testament, the tie between Passover and the Supper or any one of several other sermon or adult education series can help the congregation see the importance of this for themselves.

A. An Eight Session Series of Devotions for Elders and Deacons the Sacraments

Luke 24:13-35; John 6:35-56; Romans 6:1-13; 1 Corinthians 11:23-26

One aspect of the Church that is not emphasized today in any material that describes church growth or the personal growth of believers, either spiritually or numerically, is the sacraments. No mention can be found in the most popular book on the market, *"Worship Evangelism,"* by Sally Morgenthaler, nor is there any mention of the sacraments and their place in worship in *"Emerging Worship"* by Dan Kimball. Obviously, this is not an exhaustive list, but what it shows is the need to focus on something the Church has neglected for nearly five hundred years and to our detriment.

The word sacrament means roughly, an outward sign that has an inward significance. Augustine was the first to use the term as it is not found in scripture to mean, an outward and visible sign of an inward and spiritual grace. Augustine found in scripture over thirty ceremonies that were designated sacramenta or signs of God's inner working. The Reformers sharpened the definition by adding the phrase," as ordained by Christ our Lord in the Gospel." By this definition there were then two but essentially three; the Word of God as written and spoken (and therefore discipline as a mark of the Church), Baptism and the Lord's Supper. The power of the sacrament is in its close attachment to the Word of God. That being the case, the challenge to us is to understand what the sacraments are and how they interact with us; how God works in and through these signs and significant actions of God's work and presence in our lives.

The sacraments have power in association with the Word of God and in their effective use as a part of the body of Christ. The sacraments as we know and understand them are not solo activities but belong to and are a part of the covenant family of God. In each of the passages above the biblical context is is communal and strongly vertical, that is from God to us.

1. **Luke 24:13-35**

It was during the time of the feast of Passover and after the event of the cross. Two disciples of Jesus, make their way home after the defeat of the cross. In their despair, another joins them. The narrative of the mighty acts of God as evidenced through the patriarchs and in the writings of Moses and the prophets is recounted by Jesus, reflecting His life and ministry, His death and the story of His resurrection but told by unreliable women, yet substantiated by the disciples. Jesus opens the word to them through Himself the living Word. They are fascinated to the degree that they invite this guest, still yet unknown to them, to have supper with them. Then the key passage." When he was at the table with them, he took bread, gave thanks, broke it, and began to give it to them. Then, the disciples' eyes were opened to not only who Jesus is, but what God's will has been through the past week, and they recognized him, and he disappeared from our sight. They asked each other, "Were not our hearts burning within us while he talked with us on the road and opened the scriptures to us?"

   A. What happens at the table and in the Lord's Supper, when the bread is broken for us? Why do you think that is?
   B. What role do the breaking of the bread and the word of God have together? Which makes the other effective? Why?
   C. What is the result of their seeing?

2. **John 6:35-56**

Early in the chapter Jesus feeds the multitude with bread multiplied. In vs. 35 Jesus declares himself the bread of life. The discourse between vs.

35 and 40 reflect not only a contemporary sense of newness of life and a relationship with God, "Him I will never drive away", but also a powerful hope for the future," I shall lose none of all that he has given me but raise them up at the last day." Jesus is the bread that came down from heaven and as such is the dividing line between those who believe and those who doubt or disbelieve. Verse 53 becomes even more explicit, "Unless you eat the flesh of the son of man and drink his blood you have no life in you." The equating of life and hope are now explicitly united to the work of Jesus and who He is, the Son of God and the Son of Man, God's own, the Savior and Lord of all creation.

    A.   What is the sign here and to what does it point?

    B.   There is the equation of the manna in the wilderness to Jesus. How often did the people partake of the manna? What significance can this have for us?

3. **Romans 6:1-13**

    Paul's understanding of the nature of humanity and our own sinfulness comes out in his expression of the sacrament of baptism. The sign is the water which symbolizes the blood of Christ's atoning work on the cross. The cooperation of blood in washing and in drinking provides the conjunction of both signs and what they testify to in the life of the believer. The sign of baptism is new life, and the sign of the Lord's supper is new life. Just as all have died through Adam, now all who believe in Christ as Song of God, Lord and savior, are made alive through Jesus and His work. The washing with the blood and the opportunity to take part in the blood, both point to that work of God on our behalf. Paul discusses this more fully in his letter to the Galatians regarding circumcision and a new life we have in Jesus.

    A.   What is the solution for sin and death?

    B.   In what fashion do we see the sign of baptism presented here and how it is this sign tied together with the other sacraments?

    C.   How does celebrating this aspect of the sacrament offer hope, grace, and power to live daily?

4. **1 Corinthians 11:23-26**

Paul's discussion in 1 Corinthians is in the context of a deeply divided Church over a myriad of issues. His instruction for the Lord's Supper are given in the context of discipline and judgment. Their understanding of the gathering of believers is not one of unity but disunity, not of harmony but discord, not one of love and service but of authority and arrogance. The message of the supper can be found in verse 26 in this context where Paul says, "whenever you eat of this bread and drink of this cup you proclaim the Lord's death until he comes." The central issue for Paul is the proclamation or living out of the Lord Jesus who is in us. This is not a solo activity or private worship but a sign in the body of the Body of Christ. The sacrament is tied to Jesus' presence in the Spirit and of His ability to transform us from what we have been, our own desires and impulses, our sinful human nature, to what God has called us to be.

A. Why do we do examinations then each time we come together as a body? Why is confession critical to the body of Christ?
B. What is the source of transformation, life, and hope?

Devotions for Council

The Lord's Supper as a celebration of a wedding feast

Psalm 23:5; John 2:1-11; Revelation 19:1-9

The image of weddings is common in the bible though actual descriptions of marriage are scarce. The image of the bride and bridegroom are most frequent in the Old Testament in Psalm 45 and the Song of Songs. Psalm 23 provides an image that closely resembles the wedding image on the table that is set before the psalmist. In the wedding ceremonies and table meetings in the Old Covenant there is a sense of extravagant joy and sensory richness. The imagery of the Song of Songs is one eager expectation, and the sense of fullness and fulfillment that a wedding feast represents.

There is in both the old and new testaments a sense of heightened celebration, joy, and ceremony. John 2:1-11 captures this lavish and extravagant celebration. The wedding image was a ceremony that signaled the blessing of the community the legal union in covenant before God and a public profession of single-minded devotion. It is in this context that we can understand the imagery of the wedding feast which is given in Revelation 19:1-9.

John describes the perfect joining of the Passover with the cross in the image of the wedding used by other writers to express the salvation and expectancy of Jesus coming again. The wedding for John is this event that is a metaphor for the relationship of God with His people Here we see God as the one who chooses believers to be His bride. Jesus is to be and seen as the bridegroom of His bride, the Church, the body of Christ. John the Baptist calls himself the friend of the groom, John 3:22-30. Jesus explains his disciples lack of fasting by saying, "can the wedding guests fast while the bridegroom is with them? If they have the bridegroom with them, they cannot fast." [7]

Christ's second coming is described as a feast which points us toward Revelation 19:1-9. This consummation of Jesus with His saints at the Parousia or of His coming again, is painted for us as a wedding banquet between Christ, (the lamb of God), and his followers, His bride, the Church. "Blessed are those who are invited to the wedding supper of the Lamb", Rev. 19:9. When we think about communion and think of it as the feast that is prepared for us and the supper that awaits us, when we see ourselves in a committed relationship to Christ, and then the meal is Jesus Himself we begin to get a fuller picture of the Lord's supper.

PSALM 23:5

The lamb and the shepherd. The Lord provides for all my needs and concerns. This shepherd himself restores my soul. There is nothing that can detract from this relationship with this shepherd. The table he sets he places before me during the trials of life and during the direst of circumstances. This table is prepared for me in much the same fashion as the banquet in Revelation.

1. What does it mean to be a guest at a well thought out and supplied banquet?

2. Who lays out the food and what is the expected result?

PSALM 45

This psalm describes the extravagance that God lays out for us each day and throughout our lives. Note the gifts that have been given and remember that these occur at the banquet of the king as he weds the bride. Note then our stature as the bride of Christ and our place at the table of the king during the banquet. When we consider the Lord's Supper, who are we and what place do we hold?

---

[7]   Leland Ryken, General ed., *Dictionary of Biblical Imagery,* InterVarsity Press, pg., 938.

1. What is the nature of the character of the bride as she awaits the bridegroom? Vs. 13-14

2. What is the place of the rest of the guests and of the family that take part in this wedding feast?

JOHN 2:1-11

The new wine of the wedding represents the newness of the Spirit that is present and the emptiness of the pharisaical tradition. Let us add to that the understanding that in this setting of a wedding feast we find the best and the finest being given so that all may enjoy it. The wine, reminiscent of the cup is not like any that precede it. When do we come to the table do, do we realize in what we take part?

1. In what fashion has God saved the best for last for you?

2. When you take the cup what blessings beyond your expectations did you take part in?

REVELATION 19:1-9

The culmination of this feast mentality is the wedding feast of the lamb (Jesus Christ) and His Church. Here we see all those who have been covered by the blood of the spotless lamb, Jesus, being brought into that great feast in the same fashion of Psalm 23 and 45. To sit at the wedding of the lamb for all things are now ready gave that Church confidence in the face of the persecution of the day.

1. How does the Lord's Supper portray the hope of the coming of and completion of creation in Christ?

2. How do you understand the concept of the covenant family, the Church and the Lord's Supper? Who is there with Jesus?

Devotions for Council

The Lord's supper as the pouring out of the cup of God's Wrath

Isaiah 51:17-23; Zechariah 12:1-14; Matthew 26:36-39; Revelation 14:8-19, 16:1-19

For biblical writers, what gives a cup significance is not the appearance but what it holds.[8] A cup may therefore hold either blessing or curse. The curse may even include death, which we see in the garden of Gethsemane passage.

The image of the cup of God's wrath carries special horror because drinking it, (unlike battle, earthquake, or plague) is something a person does deliberately. In several of the passages about the cup of God's wrath we see sinners start out as arrogant (see Psalm 75:4; Jeremiah 49:12-16) but lose any vestige of human dignity as they drink the cup that God hands them.[9]

Jesus repeatedly uses the image of cup to point to his own death. He deliberately drinks of the cup not because of God's wrath on him but to take the wrath of God on Himself in place of the people who should drink of this cup! Because Jesus drinks of this cup, he can offer his followers the cup of the new covenant. This new cup is the cup of the new covenant for many for the forgiveness of sins. He drinks of the wrath so we may drink of forgiveness, compassion, and the mercy of God.[10]

---

[8]   Leland Ryken, *Dictionary of Biblical Imagery,* pg. 186.

[9]   Ibid., pg. 186.

[10]   Ibid., pg. 186.

ISAIAH 51:17-23

The cup that Israel deliberately drank in the sins of her people, has now been handed over to another who will drink of it that they should never again. The wrath of God is symbolically poured out on His people and upon those who have hurt and damaged His people. The cup points to God's judgment not only on His elect but also all humanity and indeed all creation. It is in this fashion that Paul points in Romans to God's coming to rectify and reconcile all creation to Himself.

1. What does it mean to you to be responsible for the wrath of God and deserving of it?

2. When you come to the table how does knowing that the wrath of God has been taken from you equip you to enjoy communion with God through Jesus Christ more readily?

ZECHARIAH 12:1-14

The prophet points to the destruction of the people who have oppressed Israel, from within or without. The challenge is for us to understand that those who are made to drink of this cup are the ones who has been opposed to Israel, God's people. In that same fashion we see that Zechariah now refers to the one who is to be pierced for the people, for us a direct allusion to Jesus. The one who will be pierced is the same one who drank the cup completely and yet by His blood we are set free.

1. In what fashion does partaking of the blood of Christ, make us like God vs. 8?

2. What does God pour out on the people of God? Vs. 10

MATTHEW 26:17-30,36-39

In the institution of the Lord's Supper through Matthew's eyes, we see Jesus points to the cup again as a drinking of what God has prepared for him. The proximity of the cup narrative in the garden with the institution of the supper enables us to see how Jesus teaches and prepares the disciples to understand what is about to take place for them. Let this cup pass from me is the plea of one who has set his face to Jerusalem to conduct the work of God yet knowing the full and impressive weight of what is about to happen. The drinking of the cup of God's wrath will be done, not for Him, but for his disciples and all humanity.

1. How does the supper enable us to drink the cup like Jesus for the sake of others?

2. What is the cup that you drink when you dine with God at his table?

REVELATION 14:8-19,16:1-19

Here we see in the culmination of God's revelation to His people, the sound of hope amid despair. This end times expression of the grace of God to those whom He has called and enabled to be a part of His family and judgment on the world that has fallen in sin come in one magnificent and extraordinary move, the drinking of the cup. The cup of wrath which is poured out and the winepress of God's wrath is pressed, and judgment fills the earth. Those who stand apart from the grace of God and have not drunk the cup of service and humility, of salvation and forgiveness will now drink a bitter drink indeed.

1. How does the Church and you in particular express your obedience in following Jesus?

to the point of the cup of blessing and wrath on the table?

2. What needs to change for the church and for you personally, to not be in the "winepress" of God's wrath and to be covered by His blood?

Council Devotions

The Lord's Supper as an extension of and fulfilled presence of Passover to the New Israel of God the Church

Exodus 12:1-11; Deut. 16:1-17; Luke 22:7-32 especially 30-32

The beauty of the Passover celebration and its parallel in the New Testament and its meaning for us as we look at the Lord's supper are on two separate levels. The first is the tie between the spotless lamb slaughtered to cover the people and then devoured as a sign of faith so that the people can be released from bondage and slavery. The second is the tie to the anointing of priests as holy to the Lord. [11] There are two texts that point out this similarity. Exodus 29 and Leviticus 8 point in numerous major ways to these acts of Exodus 12.

Let us be clear about the theology of the Passover and its implications to the people of Israel in their participation in it. If we understand what it means to them to whom it is written, we can begin to more clearly understand the meaning for us today. The sacrifice of the animal atones for the sin of the people, the blood sprinkled on the doorframes purifies those within, and the eating of the sacrificial meat sanctifies those who consume it. Overall, through the corporate act and participation in all its acts, the people are set free, released, and redeemed by the miracle and presence of God. By taking part in the Passover ritual, the people consecrate themselves as a nation to God, (cf. Exodus 19:6).[12]

---

[11]   Leland Ryken, *Dictionary of Biblical Imagery,* pg. 629.

[12]   Ibid., pg. 630

Understanding the crucifixion of Jesus and the subsequent resurrection add meaning and value to this sign and image. We now understand that the spotless lamb, (which will be considered under a separate heading) has been given for us, and that through His death and resurrection we now have life and have it in abundance. The supper in which we also partake in his blood, (as with the smearing of the blood on the doorposts to cover the people), and to eat the whole roasted lamb, (as with eat my body and drink my blood), enable us to take part fully in the death and life of Jesus in like fashion to the first Passover.

EXODUS 12:1-11

The core teaching and meaning derived from Passover can be located in Ex. 12.1-30. The challenge to the people of the Passover event was one of faith. They had seen the workings of God through the course of numerous miraculous events and now one more time they were to trust God with their lives. In the Lord's Supper what we have is an opportunity by faith to trust our very lives to God. As related above there are several implications of the Passover for God's people not least of which is the final and all-encompassing freedom, release from bondage, an opportunity for renewal and revival that only God can supply and that only through sacrifice. The question for us is do we believe it?

1. In thinking about Passover what is it that the people expected God to do?

2. How is this symbol effective in reminding them of God's activity in their lives?

DEUTERONOMY 16:1

Here is the explanation of God's redemptive act and as seen in a retrospective fashion. What the people are to do is remember for an entire week, to hold festival but a special kind of festival not of the celebratory nature of the wedding feast but of a more solemn nature remembering what God had done for them. The significance of the timing and the precision about the actions should remind us of what we do when we come before God's table. It is not, here a matter of frequency but intensity, a time to remember who God is and what He has done.

1. What is it you recall about communion after the fact?

2. Is there a manner of celebrating that we are missing that would enhance your appreciation of and understanding of the Lord's supper?

LUKE 22:7-38

This is one gospel account of the Last Supper celebration. Hardly celebratory. What we see here is Jesus sharing with His disciples the instructions not with an eye to setting precedent for the future generations of believers but with an eye to what is about to transpire in His life. The question which was in the forefront of the disciple's mind was why you are doing this and what does it mean as you deviate even a bit from the Passover celebration that we were expecting. And what do you mean when you say you will not do this again till the kingdom comes? The challenge to us as modern-day disciples is to understand the setting as the new Israel of God first so we can better appreciate what Jesus does for us as His Church today.

1. What is the centermost attitude of the Lord's Supper according to Luke? Vs. 27

2. As the host of this meal how is Jesus different here from what John says in Revelation 19 at the wedding feast of the lamb and the Church?

Council Devotions

The Lord's Supper as Feeding God's People

Exodus 16:31; John 6:25-40; 1 Corinthians 10:1-5; Revelation 2:1-7

"The word manna awakens sensuous images of a heaven-sent food whose literal and symbolic references enrich the bible."[13] The very name of it invites the people of God to taste touch and smell and see that the Lord is good, His gifts delicious nutritious, abundant, and free, unearned and undeserved. The image of manna as a part of the Lord's supper understanding is abundantly post-modern in its sensate presentation to God's people. As the bread of life parallels this in the Lord's supper there is this fine sense of the totality of what it means to be human wrapped up in this gift that God has given. There is one sense missing after we thoroughly understand that this substance tasted like wafers with honey, that the appearance was of a fine flake like substance, its smell when hoarded was of bred worms and became foul, its touch when the people would go about and gather it and grind it beat it or boil it and make cakes with it; is only the sense of sound. The experience of Manna is also met when we read of the people's complaints when they realize this is what they have.

Also, there is a distinct parallel here to the Lord's supper when we consider what gifts God has provided. To see the glory of Jesus, to touch him and to feel His touch, to taste and see if what God has given is not good, bring us into God's immediate presence. To complain about having to do the liturgy or prayers or come before the table more frequently because it takes away from whatever else we would like to be doing in worship or elsewhere or it takes too much time, reflects our desire that we would rather eat something else.

---

[13]   Leland Ryken, *Dictionary of Biblical Imagery,* pg. 534.

EXODUS 16

The manna is white and tasted like wafers with honey. White the symbol of purity, and the sweet taste of honey remind us of the bread as white as snow that is the body of Jesus and the taste of his presence and gift as sweet as honey. A person cannot store up God's blessings and grace. God's blessings to His people are made new for us every morning. There is enough only for each day. The tragedy of all this with relation to our view and understanding of the supper is that the people ate of it for a generation but grew tired of it. They grumbled and complained about the provision and providence of God. Surely there must be more.

1. What other things do we want rather than participate in the Lord's supper?

2. In what fashions do we attempt to store up the graces of God in this celebration?

JOHN 6:25-40

Jesus equating his own body to the experience of God's people enables us to tie this event in the Old Testament to the singular event of the Lord's supper. In 6:30-31 we see Jesus making the connection between the manna that gave life and hope to His people with His own presence and His own body that will give life and hope to His people. Jesus points out that it was God not Moses that provided for the people. Sometimes our focus shifts to what we want and what we like and who provides these things rather than the God who is the gift and the giver of the gift.

1. If Jesus is the bread of life and if manna as the symbol of that bread of life was necessary every day, how should we view the Lord's Supper in this context?

2. What other things do we tend to substitute for Jesus?

1 CORINTHIANS 10:1-5

Just briefly, we look at Paul's understanding of this whole exodus event as it pertains to God's interaction with His people. From the baptismal parallel of passing through the waters to the salvation of God and the symbols of that providence in the water, spiritual drink and spiritual food, (manna), we see Paul being very careful to lay out the word and work of God on behalf of His people that will call the church at Corinth back its first love and understanding, Jesus. The stories with symbols of the rock, the water, the bread, the spiritual drink, were all Jesus to Paul. Nevertheless, the people of Israel continued to try to do things their own way and in departing from God and His grace and will, found themselves lost and dying in the wilderness. The Lord's supper is the remedy for that lostness and death for us the same as it was for them. In the next chapter then the admonition is that as often as you do this do so in remembrance of me. So daily a sense of God's presence and provision can and should be ours through the sign and symbol of the Lord's supper.

1. What happened to the people of Israel when they disobeyed and walked away from a relationship with God? Is that true today?

2. What is the sign of that willingness to walk with God in true communion?

REVELATION 2:17

This text has been added to the study, since it completes the revelation of God and what he has done for his church. The church at Pergamum, where Satan has his throne should speak eloquently to us today. In this section where John mentions the manna that gives life and the stone that is white reminding the Church of the rock of Christ and of the gifts of God's grace, also says that there is something he holds against them. What it comes down to is that the Church is compromising with the world, allowing the world's standards values and culture to permeate the Church so that it becomes indistinguishable from the world to whom they are to witness. Put simply, this group of people in the Church said that it was possible for the Church to be like the world in many if not all ways and still be the Church of Christ.

1. In what ways has the church abandoned being Christ's Church and gone to being like the world? Do not confuse human traditions for biblical and spiritual heritage.

2. Make a list of what needs to transpire to bring the Church back to its heritage of God's church.

Council devotions

The Lord's Supper as a sign of the New Covenant

Jeremiah 31:31-34; Matthew 26:28; Heb. 8; 12:22-24

The image of covenant is the primary way the scriptures portray the relationship between God and man and more specifically to his chosen people. The covenant that for our purposes we are going back to, is one that we will look at further next month, is the covenant of God made with Abram/Abraham in Genesis 12:1-3,15:1-3,17:12-21 and confirmed in Genesis 22:1-19. It is by this covenant that all the nations of the earth will be blessed. It is to this covenant that Jeremiah points in Jeremiah 31. The action and imagery of the covenant is graphic and essential for our understanding of the Lord's supper. The exact term Berith means to cut a covenant and comes from the central action of sacrifice. A bull would be cut from head to tail in half. The blood left in between would be the field in which the covenant was sworn and then kept. The two parties of the covenant would proceed barefoot through the blood and entrails toward each other swear their covenant and then seal the deal by bending over, dipping their hands in the blood and grasping each other on their "upper thigh". [14] In a real sense by the giving of a life and by holding fast to the future of each other, they have sworn an oath that abides for all time. It is in this context that we understand the four texts above.

---

[14]   Leland Ryken, *Dictionary of Biblical Imagery,* pg. 177, and Francis Brown, S.R. Driver, C.A Briggs, *Hebrew and English Lexicon,* pg. 136,137.

JEREMIAH 31:31-34

Here we have allusion to the bride and bridegroom once again as well as the events of Exodus. The concept that surrounds all of this is the law of God, written on tablets of stone but now is written on the hearts of people. They will be able through the inner working of the Holy Spirit to understand and live following Him. The means to this grace is forgiveness of sin. The action of this grace is sacrifice and that points us to the Lord's supper as the sign of God's work in their lives.

1. What was the problem with the old covenant? Why a new one?

2. They will all know me points to a new sense of the Lord's Supper. How is it that people can know the Lord according to this passage?

MATTHEW 26:17-30

Jesus fills the meaning of the Jeremiah passage in this text. "This is my blood of the covenant which is poured out for the many for the forgiveness of sins," vs. 26. The covenant finds its fullest meaning and expression through Jesus Christ. What came before was a shadow of what is now in Him. The old covenant required the yearly sacrifice and many others to make sure the people had taken care of their guilt before God. Now in Jesus, the promise and work of God for our salvation now and forever and our empowerment by His Spirit, is finished, once for all. The new covenant is not once for some or many times for all. It has been done for us in the blood of the Lamb of God, for the people of God. The Lord's Supper should recall that we belong to that people of God, the people of the lamb.

1. Describe the ways in which Jesus fulfills the old covenant in Himself?

2. How can the Lord's supper remind you of this great sacrifice for you?

HEBREWS 8

For seven chapters the writer of Hebrews has been attempting to give understanding to the person of Jesus Christ and how He has fulfilled the Old Testament expectations of God's people. The writer of Hebrews has given this sacrifice a new meaning in the church. The point is this he says, "We have a high priest who sat down at the right hand of the throne of the majesty in heaven and who serves in the sanctuary, the true tabernacle set up the Lord, not be man," vs. 1-2. This high priest does not serve a term nor make atonement for himself. This high priest is Jesus far superior to any of the old covenant and the promise fulfilled in him better than any of the old promises. Then using the best of yelamadenu homily, the writer proves his point from the Old Testament. Jesus is the fulfillment of the law, the sacrifice, the tabernacle of worship, and of the promises. The Lord's supper is the pre-eminent sign of this fulfillment. When we participate, we are in the temple, by Jesus side, and partaking of His gifts to us.

1. What do you see when you come to the table? What are you able to see there?

2. In and through Jesus we can live out the new life and hope God gives. What can and should that mean to you today?

HEBREWS 12:14-24

This passage reinforces that the things talked about to this point are not empty ritual or vain religious activities but have within them the transformative power of God. This is a challenge to the readers of this letter to live holy lives for without that holy living people are unable to see God. Being part of this great body, the Church we now stand in an extensive line of witnesses to the grace power and presence of God. Through the individual and better yet the corporate witness of the body of Christ, the good news of the new covenant advances and enriches not only those who participate but the world in which they live.

1. What is the consequence of the Lord's supper, the work of Jesus done for us?

2. Is this effect primarily personal or does it concern all of us?

Council Devotions

The Lord's Supper is a communion in His Blood

Genesis 17:9-14, 22:8-14; John 8:31-41; 1 Corinthians 11:17-34

The image of blood is both graphic and from one point of view at least profoundly negative. Blood is the symbol for human life. Flesh and blood, blood and water remind us of our perishable nature, and both have a presence in the cross. The blood of Christ can see as both death and the means of cleansing. To bleed to death is to watch the life of God pass from one. The power of someone else's blood perceived as guilt as with Lady MacBeth in Shakespeare's writing. To have someone's blood on your hands is to stand guilty. The blood stains cannot be washed out or permanently removed by our work or anyone else's. Blood is an impurity and so a person needed cleansing to rejoin the covenant people if they had bled in any profuse manner. Point of fact is that Isaiah can find no image more abhorrent than comparing all our righteous deeds to menstrual rags (Isa.64:6).[15] Since blood carries all these negative connotations, it also is how God makes propitiation or atonement for the guilt and sin of man. It is against that backdrop that we more fully understand the blood of the covenant.

---

[15]   Leland Ryken, *Dictionary of Biblical Imagery,* pg. 100.

GENESIS 17:9-14,22:8-14

Chapter 17 is prologue to the main event upcoming in chapter 22. Here we see the promise of God attendant by the sign in blood of initiation into the covenant, circumcision. Blood is a very real part of circumcision, and through it the person(people) was reminded of the promise of God and of our covenant responsibility to Him. All those who fell under the influence of God's covenantal people were to bear the sign. It would remind all that God had made promises and would be faithful to them. This covenant is tested when God calls Abraham to sacrifice his only son, who he thinks is the hope of the nations, or at least certainly Abraham's tribe of nations. Here we see God provide the sacrifice, a foreshadowing of Jesus work in the cross for us in the cross event.

1. What do we use today that has the intensity and depth of feeling and meaning as the blood did for Abraham?

2. God sees the totality of our lives and others every day. To whom do we usually look for the sacrifice?

JOHN 8:31-41

This passage in John parallels and mirrors the discussion in Genesis. There would have been little doubt about what Jesus was saying to the Jews here. The contrast between the absence of power in the mere sign of circumcision and the power of Jesus presence to them is quite clear. "If you were Abraham's children then you would do the things Abraham did." Habakkuk 2:4, and Paul's use of it in Romans 1:17 and Galatians 3:11, reminds us that Abraham believed God and His right standing with God according to Habakkuk was the Abraham was reckoned to God as righteousness. What Abraham did we too must do and the means to that end is the person of Jesus Christ? The Lord's supper then as sign and seal of both Jesus and the event of the cross, enable us to live by the Spirit in obedience to Him through a faith and grace that does not belong to us but are a gift from God.

1. What is the sign of belonging to God according to Jesus?

2. What does it mean to you that the righteous shall live by faith and how is that pertinent to the Lord's supper?

1 CORINTHIANS 11:17-34

Paul picks up where John left off in John 8. There is no commendation for a Church that mishandles the sacrifice of God for them. Here we see a Church torn by division and dissension. The people who come together are neither one with Jesus in fellowship through communion nor with each other in Spirit. They are each self-righteous in their own eyes and so when they come to the table each feels ample ground to come on their own terms. Here we see Paul go back to the basic biblical imagery for blood being death, guilt, and impurity and even as an omen of the impending doom they bring on themselves if they persist in such a manner. We made this a very individualistic challenge in our preparatory service when Paul meant it to be an admonition to the Church. Certainly, body of Christ or Church preparation is preceded by individual, but it can't be left to the individual.

1. What groups or areas in our Church need addressing before we come to the table again?

2. In what ways are you coming to the table in a self-righteous manner?

Council Devotions

The Lord's Supper and the Lamb of God Who Takes Away the Sins of the World

Genesis 22:8; Exodus 29:39; Isaiah 53:7; John 1:29-36; Revelation 5:6-12

The image of a lamb as part of the flock is plentiful in a rural, agrarian society. The meaning and impact associated with the lamb of the flock is not usually one of, being led to slaughter, one of innocence, gentleness, and dependence. This image of the of the lamb is transferred to the servant of God in Isa. 53:7 and used of that lamb led to slaughter in Jer. 51:40.

Even more numerous are the passages that associate the lamb with sacrifice specifically. Lambs are specifically mentioned in this connection more than eighty times in Exodus, Leviticus and Deuteronomy combined.[16] This lamb finds its perfect analogy in Jesus, who according to Peter in 1 Peter 1:19 is like a lamb without defect or blemish, mentioned by Paul in 1 Corinthians 5:7 as the paschal (suffering) lamb, and by John the Baptist in John as the lamb of God who takes away the sins of the world.

GENESIS 22:8; EXODUS 29:39

The foundation for understanding Jesus as the sacrifice to God by faith for our sins is presented in God's word for His people here. With the sacrifice provided by God, Abraham cannot give thanks to God for His

---

16   Leland Ryken, *Dictionary of Biblical Imagery,* InterVarsity Press, pg. 484.

abundant gift but also see the fulfillment of the hope he has not only for his tribe but for the nations. Abraham's sacrifice to God finds acceptance and leads to the fuller understanding in the context of the exodus event. The spotless lamb is sign of God's judgment passing over His called-out people. The blood sacrifice and the eating of the flesh point to Jesus and the event of the cross. The Lord's supper should remind us of God's providence but also the suffering, and death that is involved for our freedom.

1. Why does the image of a spotless lamb being killed stir up such emotion for the people of Israel? What about in us today?

2. The image of the lamb led to slaughter holds little meaning for us. Why?

ISAIAH 53:7; JEREMIAH 51:40

The prophetic image reminded the people of God as to their responsibility to be the witness and instrument of the salvation of the world. It was by their sacrifice of their own rights and privileges that they would be able to reflect to the world the grace, power, and presence of God. The people were unable and unwilling to obey. The texts above are Old Testament signposts to the one who would come and fulfill all righteousness for all humanity.

1. How can we today having the mind of Christ in us be that lamb who is dumb and being led to slaughter?

2. Are we willing to give up all our rights and prerogatives for the sake of others that they may find the grace, peace and presence of God? How can we show this?

JOHN 1:29-36; REVELATION 5:6-12

John's relating of John the Baptist's understanding of Jesus is prelude to his presentation of Jesus in the Revelation. Jesus is the lamb of God that takes away the sins of the world. He is now that sacrifice that God gave to Abraham, to Moses and the people of Israel and now to the world through the medium of the cross. When we come to the table, we are accompanying an extensive line of faithful people who have participated by faith in the righteousness of God. When we come to the table it is both a gift given to us and a proclamation of God's grace to the world through us.

1. What special gift is this lamb given according to John in Revelation 5 and how does that relate to the table and communion?

2. What has this lamb become and how does that inform our understanding of communion?

IX

Sample Devotions

In this chapter you will find several examples of devotions not in Church year order. I did not attempt to put them in church year order, personal preference or usage order. The intention was for you to be able to develop the three separate projects, liturgy for examination the week before, devotions for that span of time between examination and celebration and the liturgy for the celebration that shares the theme and reinforces that theme through the formulary in that liturgy. These few examples are given to give you an idea as to how it might look for you as you engage in this practice in your own worship experience.

You may use these devotions and liturgies for the celebration, complete in their current form, you may adapt and adopt them for your own usage or merely use them for ideas to form your own devotions and liturgies. My hope is that you will explore the scriptures for yourself. This is not only for self-edification but also should enable you to write devotions for your own congregation that will benefit them where they are geographically but also in terms of what their culture and society look like at that moment in time. There are no liturgies printed here for the Sunday before celebration for self-examination.

This collection should give you a good head start for your own preparation for a more frequent celebration of communion. It can give you an emergency backlog to reference when the pressures of the ministry prohibit you from writing your own. It is my fondest hope that it will most of all spur you to new heights of creativity and theological and biblical discovery in your own life to enable you to more deeply and passionately know our Lord and follow Him.

Body of Christ Communion Devotions and Liturgy

Sunday -Exodus 12:27-you shall say, 'It is the sacrifice of the Lord's Passover, for he passed over the houses of the people of Israel in Egypt, when he struck the Egyptians but spared our houses.'" And the people bowed their heads and worshiped.

What strikes me in this passage is the universal gift of God for the people of God. The gift is first, faith to believe. Then the gift is obedience to live. Then the gift is joy in salvation. At this first Passover, this first table of the Lord, all God's people, are invited, those who have faith in God's power and presence, the true Israel of God, to attend the feast of the lamb. Those who believe in the work of God through grace by faith, are blessed in this promise of God as a sign of His gift of faith by and in the work of God. If we read further, those who do not believe by God's grace, and do not reflect that faith in obedience to Him in deeds that reflect belief in Him, are condemned by God. To be a part of the body of Christ, of the family of God, God truly blesses us by the invitation to the meal and our participation in it.

Thought: this week, what does it mean to be invited to the feast and to be a part of the Body of Christ, the family of God?

Monday - 2 Kings 23:21-22 ²¹ And the king commanded all the people, "Keep the Passover to the Lord your God, as it is written in this Book of the Covenant." ²² For no such Passover had been kept since the days of the judges who judged Israel, or during all the days of the kings of Israel or of the kings of Judah.

"The king commanded all the people, keep the Passover of the Lord your God." All the people! Again, we see here the universality of the gift of God for the people of God. There is a condition, obedience. The people of God will be a people of the covenant, they will be a people who worship Yahweh, the Lord God and Him alone. They will be a people who will be a body, they will care for the others around them who are created in God's image. Those who do these things are welcome to the table to fed by, saved by, and provided for by God. This week we have a chance to remember others in the congregation and the life of this body we share with God and each other.

Prayer: Lord and Father God, help us to experience our uniting with you and each other in obedience to your command and will. Amen

Tuesday - Ezra 6:20-21 [20] *For the priests and the Levites had purified themselves together; all of them were clean. So, they slaughtered the Passover lamb for all the returned exiles, for their fellow priests, and for themselves.* [21] *It was eaten by the people of Israel who had returned from exile, and by everyone who had joined them and separated himself from the uncleanness of the peoples of the land to worship the Lord, the God of Israel.*

"...they slaughtered the lamb for all the exiles." The body of Christ remains in exile. As the church we are sojourners and aliens in a foreign land. This is not our home. When we come to the table, we remember by God through His Word and prophets, that the table has been prepared for us by God, provided for us in God, and positioned us to walk with God. Prepared, provided, and positioned not by our own desires, will and efforts but by the work and will of God alone. Coming to the table as a church, a body, a family this week should remind us that we all belong to Him by His grace and for His glory. We are the body of Christ. Let us live like it!

Activity: What can you do this week as an individual, a family and with one other family from the body, which will show the care, love and encouragement a family derives from when they dine together. Think of thanksgiving meals!

Wednesday - Rom. 7:4 [4] *Likewise, my brothers, you also have died to the law through the body of Christ, so that you may belong to another, to him who has been raised from the dead, in order that we may bear fruit for God.*

What does it mean to die to the law through the body of Christ? What the law had done in Israel is drive the people apart, set up classes of people, some better, a lot worse. Instead of drawing people together to be support for and encouragement to other people they pushed away. We saw the same thing today. In the world frequently and too often in the church we use the law to drive wedges between ourselves. We are to be a new body, resurrected in the power and life of Jesus Christ. On the table is God's reminder in the manner of the manna, that the bread was given by God and broken apart so that we could be united in Him.

Thought: What ways have divided us and on what basis biblically, was that division? Does what draw us together, faith and life in the body of Christ, mean more to us than what drives us apart? Confess your own part in this, this week.

Thursday - 1 Corinthians 12:12,27 *¹² For just as the body is one and has many members, and all the members of the body, though many, are one body, so it is with Christ. ²⁷ Now you are the body of Christ and individually members of it.*

Jesus gave the new Adam, the body of Christ, for His bride the Church. Eph. 5 helps us to understand this, and we will point to that tomorrow. But for today, all we need to know is that what God pointed to through Israel that we heard about and saw through the Old Testament has become real and present in the Church today. Each of you that read this are essential and important. Not merely because you are part of the body but because you are in God's image and likeness and we are knit together in the character of Jesus Christ. The table celebration as a body is essential for this. As we gather this Sunday, it is much more than just you and yours coming to church. It is becoming one with the body of Christ.

Activity: Find new friends and new ways of being together as God's family this week by seeking out new relationships with new people.

Friday - Ephesians 4:12 *¹² to equip the saints for the work of ministry, for building up the body of Christ,*

Like all good bodies, if we eat without exercise, we get flabby. We need to work out. The work of the body of Christ is a team exercise, like a tug of war. Picture Artesia First on one side of the rope and the culture and world around us on the other. The object of the game is to get the other side onto your side. The one that does that wins! It is the goal of the body of Christ to win this "game" by pulling the world and its culture into the kingdom of God. Eating well is part of it. Come to the table. For us to be built up, let us exercise together as a team this week to bring others around us into the kingdom.

Prayer: Father, help us to exercise our spiritual life well since we have been fed well at your table. Amen

Saturday - Hebrews 10:10 *¹⁰ And by that will we have been sanctified through the offering of the body of Jesus Christ once for all.*

We can be transformed to be different is to the glory of God for the work of His kingdom. This means that work needs to be done for us by Jesus Christ. Tomorrow when you come to the table, remember that you, and that is the plural you, are set apart by God's sacrifice for the ministry of God's kingdom. The body of Christ was given for the Church, body of Christ. It is not merely something we do, it does something in and through us. When you dine tomorrow feel the Lord's presence, revel in Jesus Spirit and life and then leave empowered by that presence and Spirit to be Christ to the world around us.

Prayer: Father, remove whatever is not yet holy in my/our lives so that we may be for you, your presence in the world and may give glory to you in all we do and are. Amen

Communion Devotions-
The Blood of Jesus

Monday Genesis 22:8-14

The blood that God offers for our lives connects Christmas and Communion. This passage from Genesis is foundational for our understanding of not only what God has done for us, but also the benefit of communion for us. God's gift of the child, Isaac, and then God's subsequent gift of the ram/lamb for Isaac in fulfillment of His promise to Abraham, parallel closely God's gift to us of His Son Jesus Christ and of the subsequent gift of His Holy Spirit. Consider what the blood in Genesis 22 purchased. The purchase of an inheritance for Abraham, the future for Israel, the life of Isaac, are all at God's expense. Now consider the Church in the New Covenant. The purchase was for the Kingdom of God, the bride the Church and for you personally.

> **CHALLENGE**: As you come to communion next Sunday
> can you enlarge your vision to see the immensity of God's
> gift to you in the symbols of the cup and bread?

Tuesday Leviticus 17:10-13

Here in this text we see spelled out for us, the power of God's blood is explained by Moses, to Israel. The gift of God is blood, life for life. This gift of God cannot be taken lightly or cheaply. The very essence of who we are and what we are individually and collectively as Christ's body the Church, is held in the blood. Today's science confirms this. We frequently will hear talk about the blood evidence and DNA held in those tiny scarlet drops. While each of us has different DNA, what binds us together is the life in the blood that we have in God's Spirit by God's creation. The blood of the covenant covers our sins and purges our transgressions. This is the cup of the new covenant in Jesus' blood. The blood here testifies either against or for Israel. It can be the cup of His blood of wrath against them or the cup of His wrath swallowed by God for them. The point is a life for a life. Come to the table and realize that it is God's gift of His son, a life for our life that communion is all about.

QUESTION: For whom would you give your life? What does that tell you about God and His character as well as the nature of Christmas?

Wednesday Hebrews 13-14,19-26

Blood purifies? Have you ever gotten a cut and then smeared it on a white shirt or blouse? The blood damages the garment by the stain of the blood if not ruined permanently; if not purified by some other agent powerful enough to make it clean. To purify is to make clean, to wipe away. Blood spoils and marks, it damages beyond repair. But God turns things upside down. Blood here provides the hope of forgiveness. Blood provides life in the death of the giver, Jesus Christ. Blood provides covering for our sins not a stain without end. Think about this passage and the communion we are about to enjoy together. Think about God's gift of His son and what Christmas really means. When you take the cup on Sunday can you see the blood of God's Son given for you? Then can you feel the life of Christ course through your veins as you live anew through Him?

THOUGHT: If Jesus life indeed courses through you, how would your life look different after Sunday's communion?

Thursday Romans 3:23-26

Sin and despair, Death and discouragement, Christmas and Christ are all joined together in this supper. The rose of Sharon which is depicted and by legend assumed used for crucifixion, has thorns that draw blood. The blood of this Christmas rose provides all we need in our despair and impossible life situations. We are being redeemed, ransomed from the effects of sin and death by the blood of Jesus on the cross. Where the wages of sin is death, (among many other consequences), the gift of Christ on the cross is life and hope. Thanks be to God for the gift of Christmas which points us to the cross of Christ and the gift of hope and life.

> **CHALLENGE:** What are you feeling desperate about today, a physical condition, a mental challenge, and an attitude or habit that has a lock on you? why not give it up to Jesus this week.

Friday Colossians 1:14-20

Here is yet one more concept for which the blood of Jesus is sufficient, forgiveness. The word Paul uses here, aphesis, means to be released from bondage or imprisonment. Not only release but the remission of the penalty. If by one sin we are guilty, then also by one sacrifice are we also set free? This is Paul's point in this text which describes the Jesus we celebrate at Christmas. The greatest gift of all some say is Jesus, the reason for the season. It is not just the person of Jesus however, but the work of Jesus accomplished in the cross that stands out! The Jesus who redeems us is the Jesus through whom we were created and the same Jesus in whom we take breath each day. God has given life, recreated life and sustained life in Christ. That is the core meaning of communion. This Christmas come with a new conviction about the Christ of Christmas.

> **QUESTION:** What is the sentence that your sin requires even now? How can you express gratitude to God and appreciation to Jesus the Son because of His work at Christmas?

Saturday John 6:53-56

We are created by God's work and in His image as eternal beings. While God is eternal without creation, we require His life for our eternal life. One of the great misconceptions of heaven, hell and eternity is that we will live forever either way. What this passage makes clear is that eternity is ours either way that is true, but for those apart from the blood of Christ, it is eternal death. Understand the difference. To have life in His blood is to live fully where there are no more tears and no more sorrow. To live apart from His blood is to be eternally aware and dead to it all. When you come to the table tomorrow, come as a family of God, as a body of Christ but most of all a person in whom the life of Christ lives with all these others God has brought into your life.

> **THOUGHT:** Have you taken the time to get right with all the other people with whom God has placed you in relationship this week? What more do you need to do?

Sunday 1 Corinthians 11:17-34

These are the words of the institution we use. The cup of blessing we bless is to us the blood of Jesus. Christmas is about the blood of Christ, very God of very God, given for us. The work begins at the incarnation and ends at the resurrection. Our renewed spiritual life is confirmed as being from God through the gift of the Holy Spirit and has, for us, new meaning because of the obedience of a girl to God's will and the submission of a man to God's call. Can we do anything less? Today when you come to the table, come ready to be obedient to God and submissive to His will.

The Table of God prepared for you.

Monday- Exodus 25:23-30-

Since we are going to talk about the table, let us start at the beginning. It is God's table and there are specific instructions as to what it looks like and what is on it. The table that is prepared for us in Psalm 23:5-6 is of the same type as this table. This table is not fixed in time nor is it stationary in a certain place. It is not like any other table in any other place, the table of the Lord's Supper is separated from what is common and worldly and is holy. It has room for offerings and sacrifices and the bread is always present. That is the most crucial point; the bread is there all the time. This would have meant something to the people during the exodus. Bread was life. The table was God's, and the bread was life. And the bread is to us the body of Christ.

How do you see the table of God? What is on it and who stands behind it? What do the elements represent to you?

Tuesday- Numbers 3:27-32

We understand the table now; it is God's table, and He provides the nourishment for it. Now we see those who attend the table. The place where the table is holy. It is unlike any other place in all creation. As such those who deal with the things of this place must also be holy. They deal with the table and the service of the table with care and reverence.

As you come to the table of God, do you see it as special, holy
and in fact an opportunity to be come into God's presence
and be able to stand in that presence by the work of God?
If so, what does that mean to you and if not why?

Wednesday- 2 Samuel 9:7-13

What a privilege it is to eat at the king's table. From servant and son
of a servant to sitting and dining with the king. The food was better, the
company probably a cut above and certainly the time spent more relaxed
and rewarding. So, it is also for us when we come to the King's table. The
table set before us in the presence of our enemies is indeed the King's table.

This Sunday we are coming to the King's table. How would you act in
a different manner than you usually do when you dine? Why?

Thursday Psalm 78:18-25

Here we see people steeped in sin and filled with doubt and anxiety
wondering about the providence of God for them. The anger of God is
measured by His mercy and grace. Instead of causing judgment because of
sin and doubt, God causes the sky to rain manna. Indeed, as Jesus observes
later in John 6, this manna is the bread of life for the people who have been
set free but depend on God for their daily provision.

Do you depend on God for your daily provision in actuality?
Most of us rely on our own resources. Can you look back
and remember a time when God did indeed provide your
every need? What would it take to go back there again?

Friday- Luke 22:21-30

Who sits at the head of the table in your house? Why? The whole
table seating arrangement is critical. In most households there are places
of honor for guests and places of familiarity for those who are frequently
there. In my house growing up, the place for my mother, which was set

apart for her to sit, was closest to the kitchen. Here we see Jesus in a dispute about who gets what place at the table. His emphasis is on service and sacrifice. When you come to God's table do you see Jesus serving you and when you leave God's table do you see it as your responsibility to serve each other and others in the community?

Saturday- 1 Corinthians 10:14-22

It is interesting that Paul places the Lord's supper and table fellowship in a discussion of idolatry. Why is that? What do you think? Paul's point is the seriousness of how we approach the Lord's supper. Is not the cup of Christ a participation in the blood of Jesus? Is not the loaf a reminder that we are one body and when we partake, we are unified? When we sit down at the table, we need desperately to not only be right with the host of the meal but with all those others who are sitting down to dine with us. Are you at peace with everyone here? What can you do about it and how can God through Jesus Christ help you?

Sunday Hebrews 9:1-10

The writer of Hebrews wants us to know that the narrative of God's action done in the Old Testament was a foreshadow of what Jesus would do for us for all time and in all places. He is at the table. He is the cup. He is the bread. He is the priest. He is the source of life and the sustainer of life. As you come to the table this morning, give thanks to God that what was once shadow is now reality for you. Then come to the table and enjoy the presence of God in Spirit, Word, and Sacrament.

Devotions for The New Covenant of God

Sunday *Genesis 1:27; 3:22-23* ²⁷ *So God created man in his own image, in the image of God he created him; male and female he created them.* ²² *Then the Lord God said, "Behold, the man has become like one of us in knowing good and evil. Now, lest he reach out his hand and take also of the tree of life and eat and live forever—"* ²³ *therefore the Lord God sent him out from the garden of Eden to work the ground from which he was taken."*

While not a covenant in the strictest sense, it is a covenant of new beginnings. God creates. God blesses. God calls people into a relationship with Him. God marks out the boundaries of this new relationship. (See Genesis 1-3). God also restores and redefines the relationship after humanity transgresses the boundary. The New Beginning of creation has another new beginning with God providing for, caring for and loving His creation. That is a promise of God. This promise sees its fulfillment in the bread and the cup. The new beginning of a new creation in each of us through the work of God in Jesus Christ.

Thought: Where do you need to start new in your relationship with God this week?

Monday *Genesis 9:7-11* ⁷ *And you, be fruitful and multiply, increase greatly on the earth and multiply in it."* ⁸ *Then God said to Noah and to his sons with him,* ⁹ *"Behold, I establish my covenant with you and your offspring after you,* ¹⁰ *and with every living creature that is with you, the birds, the livestock, and every beast of the earth with you, as many as came out of the ark; it is for every beast of the earth.* ¹¹ *I establish my covenant with you, that never again shall all flesh be cut off by the waters of the flood, and never again shall there be a flood to destroy the earth."*

A covenant, a promise or an agreement was made between a victorious party and a defeated party. The defeated party pays the victorious party with their life. God has turned around the conditions of covenant. Humanity is wicked and sinful. Humanity despoils God's creation and the relationships of it. Noah becomes the source of rescue. The same words used in the creation story are used here with Noah in this creation 2.0 reboot. Does God owe humanity? Who owns the debt, God, or humanity? Yet God pays the debt for us. Now think about your life and the life of God given up for you. What is your debt? How much do you owe? Who is going to make the payoff? What would it be like for you to start over, NEW?

Activity: Make a list of what your debt to God includes just for the past 3 days. You do not have to show it to anyone. Then pray and thank God for the debt paid in the work of Jesus.

Tuesday *Genesis 12:1-3; Now the Lord said to Abram, "Go from your country and your kindred and your father's house to the land that I will show you. ² And I will make of you a great nation, and I will bless you and make your name great, so that you will be a blessing. ³ I will bless those who bless you, and him who dishonors you I will curse, and in you all the families of the earth shall be blessed." 15:7-18 ¹⁷ When the sun had gone down and it was dark, behold, a smoking fire pot and a flaming torch passed between these pieces. ¹⁸ On that day the Lord made a covenant with Abram, saying, "To your offspring I give this land, from the river of Egypt to the great river, the river Euphrates…"*

Abram became Abraham, the father of many nations. This was another new beginning. It is to Abraham that Israel looks to as a foundation, see John 8. There is a reference to Abraham as evidence for the certainty of resurrection, I am the God of the living not the dead. Our life is in God. That life exemplified in the bread and the cup, body, and blood. It is to this Jesus refers in John 8. New life for all humanity is possible through Abraham. New life for all eternity is possible through Jesus Christ. God's covenant with Abraham as Habakkuk 2:4 puts it is, "Abraham believed God and it was reckoned as righteousness." Do we believe God? Coming to the table by faith and grace is a sign of our faith in God's promise and work. Grace by faith makes us a new creation. How are you living new this week?

Thought: When you believe in something or believe in something what do you do with it?

Wednesday *Exodus 24:8 ⁸ And Moses took the blood, threw it on the people, and said, "Behold the blood of the covenant that the Lord has made with you in accordance with all these words."*

The Covenant God made with Israel clarified by the Hebrew used in Exodus 20:1. "Behold I am the Lord your God. I brought you out of the land of Egypt, out of the land of slavery. Therefore...." God's work brought freedom. God's work brought salvation. God's work brought life. In Egypt there was only work and death. With God there was grace and life. It was the blood of the lamb. Just like with Abraham and the sacrifice provided for Isaac, we see in Israel and Moses this profound act of God for the life of those who do not deserve it. That brings us to the table this week. The act of God is in the cross of Christ given for those who do not deserve it. God through the work of His Son, has brought us out of the world, has brought us out of slavery to sin, has replaced death with life in the Son. How grateful are you for the life that God has given? Here Israel gets new life. At the table you have an opportunity for a new life. Will you grasp it?

Prayer: Thank you Father for the life of your Son that we can share. Father may we never take your love for granted but always feel that gratitude of grace given, and life changed forever.

Thursday *Jeremiah 31:30-32³⁰ But everyone shall die for his own iniquity. Each man who eats sour grapes, his teeth shall be set on edge. ³¹ "Behold, the days are coming, declares the Lord, when I will make a new covenant with the house of Israel and the house of Judah, ³² not like the covenant that I made with their fathers on the day when I took them by the hand to bring them out of the land of Egypt, my covenant that they broke, though I was their husband, declares the Lord.*

Why a new covenant? What was wrong with the old one? Another new beginning. The problem with the old covenant was not in the sign but in who people trust for the work of the sign. What was happening then happens today as well. We overlook grace or take it for granted. The grace

God intends for life leads to our works which only produce death. Trusting in our own work and life leads to no confidence at all. All our lives produce death and less than satisfactory results. What would work? Quit trusting yourself and your own work and trust God. How? By grace through faith. The table gives us an opportunity to do just that. Trust God. What we do not see we believe. What we do not do God does for us. Come to the table this week, have faith that what God has done is sufficient and live by His grace. What benefit comes to you in this new covenant? Are we taking full advantage of it in Christ?

Activity: What are you currently doing that reflects your trust in your own goodness and work? Give it up to God.

Friday *John 6:53-58* ^{53} *So Jesus said to them, "Truly, truly, I say to you, unless you eat the flesh of the Son of Man and drink his blood, you have no life in you.* ^{54} *Whoever feeds on my flesh and drinks my blood has eternal life, and I will raise him up on the last day.* ^{55} *For my flesh is true food, and my blood is true drink.* ^{56} *Whoever feeds on my flesh and drinks my blood abides in me, and I in him.* ^{57} *As the living Father sent me, and I live because of the Father, so whoever feeds on me, he also will live because of me.* ^{58} *This is the bread that came down from heaven, not like the bread the fathers ate, and died. Whoever feeds on this bread will live forever."*

This is the theme of Jesus ministry. This is the key that unlocks the kingdom. This is the source of life. It has been that way since Genesis. God's WORD is the source of life. God's presence is the source of life. God's gift of Himself to us is the source of life. God breathed it into us at creation. He enabled us to sail over it in the flood. He poured it out for us in the sacrifice provided to Abraham and He showed the way by the blood of lamb for Israel. Jesus, the WORD of God who dwells with us, is our life, our hope forever. When you come to the table this Sunday, think about the WORD of God that gives life. God loved the world so much that He gave His Son. Whoever believes in me has life. I am the way, the truth, and the life. This is all God's gift to us. Receive it and follow Him from the table into the world. Too often the world is comfortable with the old way. What does God's newness offer you today?

Prayer: Father, forgive us for trusting in anything other than your Son. Forgive us for living in any way that does not follow the Son. Forgive us for those times when we put on the world rather than put on Christ. Fill us this day with your eternal Son, Jesus the Messiah, the one who saves His people from their sins. Amen

Saturday *Hebrews 6:13-18 [13] For when God made a promise to Abraham, since he had no one greater by whom to swear, he swore by himself, [14] saying, "Surely I will bless you and multiply you." [15] And thus Abraham, having patiently waited, obtained the promise. [16] For people swear by something greater than themselves, and in all their disputes an oath is final for confirmation. [17] So when God desired to show more convincingly to the heirs of the promise the unchangeable character of his purpose, he guaranteed it with an oath, [18] so that by two unchangeable things, in which it is impossible for God to lie, we who have fled for refuge might have strong encouragement to hold fast to the hope set before us.*

Covenant, promise, oath. All fit together in Jesus. Verse 18 refers to two unchangeable things. Here is the heart and soul of Communion. The promise of God and the oath of God. God's promise is life. God's oath is He is the author of that life. We live in a world where words are cheap, abused and misused all the time. God does not lie. God fulfills His promise. The bread and the wine tomorrow point to the promise of God made in Genesis and renewed and restored in Noah, Abraham, Israel and finally in Jesus. Why not start new this week and this year? It is not too late. Live by grace. Live by faith. Live in Jesus now and forever. Here is the New in the New Covenant. God makes a promise in His Son. His Son is God's Word. God takes an oath on His WORD Jesus Christ. That is something you can count on.

Activity: Re-read Heidelberg Catechism Question and Answer 1. What is God saying to you today regarding your comfort and your hope?

Advent Communion Devotions

True Eucharist: Thanksgiving to God

Monday   **Luke 10:18-22 (ESV)**

18 And he said to them, "I saw Satan fall like lightning from heaven. 19 Behold, I have given you authority to tread on serpents and scorpions, and over all the power of the enemy, and nothing shall hurt you. 20 Nevertheless, do not rejoice in this, that the spirits are subject to you, but rejoice that your names are written in heaven."21 In that same hour he rejoiced in the Holy Spirit and said, "I thank you, Father, Lord of heaven and earth, that you have hidden these things from the wise and understanding and revealed them to little children; yes, Father, for such was your gracious will.[a] 22 All things have been handed over to me by my Father, and no one knows who the Son is except the Father, or who the Father is except the Son and anyone to whom the Son chooses to reveal him."

Eucharist: Thanks be to God! Jesus in this passage offers thanks to God for something that on the surface seems strange. What has been revealed to His disciples has been hidden to those who are the spiritual and intellectual leaders of His day. How odd. You would think Jesus would reveal important things to important people, so they can explain it to others. Jesus is thankful however, that God's will and work are for all people created in His image. Our own thankfulness to God ought to be in line with Jesus. Thank God what has been hidden, is now made plain in Jesus to us!

Prayer: Thank you heavenly Father for the provision you have made for us in your Son, Jesus Christ. Amen

Paul A. Hansen

Tuesday   John 11:40-42 (ESV)

⁴⁰ Jesus said to her, "Did I not tell you that if you believed you would see the glory of God?" ⁴¹ So they took away the stone. And Jesus lifted up his eyes and said, "Father, I thank you that you have heard me. ⁴² I knew that you always hear me, but I said this on account of the people standing around, that they may believe that you sent me."

Thanks for listening! Have you ever merely been grateful that someone heard you out! In our busy world, people seldom take time to listen, let alone hear our concerns or our conversations. We are distracted people who seem to suffer frequently from cultural attention deficit disorder. The demands of work, school, neighborhood, international affairs and church can make it difficult to focus on the life God gives. Here Jesus is grateful to God for the life of His friend that is given back. He is thankful to His Father for listening to His plea. Are we grateful and thankful to God that He has listened to our plea and our needs and has given us life in the face of death due to sin and an estranged relationship? Thanks be to God!!

Activity: What would you like to take a moment to thank God for that reflects the life you have in Him today?

Wednesday   Colossians 3:15 (ESV)

¹⁵ And let the peace of Christ rule in your hearts, to which indeed you were called in one body. And be thankful.

Unity, a oneness because we are joined together as the body of Christ, is the basis of our peace. Peace is that Hebrew sense of Shalom, wholeness contentment, well-being that we have in being united with God. In the Eucharist, the thanksgiving meal, we are united with God through the body and blood of His Son Jesus Christ. For that we ought to be thankful. The Advent and Christmas season reminds us that we are all drawn together as a single body by the prince of peace, Jesus Christ. How thankful are you for that great gift?

Activity: Write a thank you note to God for all that He has given to you.

Thursday   Romans 7:21-25 (ESV)

²¹ So I find it to be a law that when I want to do right, evil lies close at hand. ²² For I delight in the law of God, in my inner being, ²³ but I see in my members another law waging war against the law of my mind and making me captive to the law of sin that dwells in my members. ²⁴ Wretched man that I am! Who will deliver me from this body of death? ²⁵ Thanks be to God through Jesus Christ our Lord! So then, I myself serve the law of God with my mind, but with my flesh I serve the law of sin.

What a wretched person I am. I just cannot get it right. Even when I try to do the right thing, wickedness lies right next to me. Why is that and what can be done about it? The reason is sin and my depraved nature. What can we do, or God do for us as sinners, Paul practically shouts in verse twenty-five. Thanks be to God. There it is again. Eucharist. Thanks be to God through the work of Jesus Christ. This Advent why not thank God for the work He has done in Jesus Christ. Think of the ministry of Jesus, healing, feeding, leading, caring, protecting humanity. Are we thankful? Think about the table. The bread and the cup should remind us of the work of Jesus for the forgiveness of sins. Are we grateful?

Activity: take a moment and write down a list of sins committed. If you are with your family do this by yourself. Then thank God for His unfailing forgiveness in your life.

Friday   2 Corinthians 9:12-15 (ESV)

¹² For the ministry of this service is not only supplying the needs of the saints but is also overflowing in many thanksgivings to God. ¹³ By their approval of this service, they will glorify God because of your submission that comes from your confession of the gospel of Christ, and the generosity of your contribution for them and for all others, ¹⁴ while they long for you and pray for you, because of the surpassing grace of God upon you. ¹⁵ Thanks be to God for his inexpressible gift!

The service we perform, which mirrors the service Jesus has performed for us, should overflow in expressions of thanks to God. Paul shares with the Corinthian Church, no model of the ideal Church, that despite who they are and how divided they are (read both letters sometime), all that they do in Jesus' name should resound in thanks to God! In fact, these works should OVERFLOW in thanks to God. When we not only confess the gospel but live it, people see Jesus and praise God. When we come to the table this week, let Jesus work there be a model for us to pattern our lives after and watch what happens as people give thanks to God and praise His name.

Action: This thanksgiving and through this next year what can you do individually or as a family to serve God? Beacon for Him, Samaritan's purse, World Renew disaster response, care for a neighbor or a family member. Pick one or two and watch what God will do.

Saturday   Revelation 7:10-12 (ESV)

[10] and crying out with a loud voice, "Salvation belongs to our God who sits on the throne, and to the Lamb!" [11] And all the angels were standing around the throne and around the elders and the four living creatures, and they fell on their faces before the throne and worshiped God, [12] saying, "Amen! Blessing and glory and wisdom and thanksgiving and honor and power and might be to our God forever and ever! Amen."

Thanks be to God through the resurrected and ascended Jesus Christ, His Son. Thanks be to God through His Son, the creator of the Universe who made all things by Him and through Him and For Him. Thanks be to God through the Spirit of Jesus Christ, who empowers and encourages His Body the Church. When it comes to giving thanks tomorrow, come to the table with a renewed sense of the joy and excitement of receiving a gift you desperately need as if for the first time. Then, after receiving it, give thanks to God like the heavenly host in this passage. Remember to praise His name and give thanks to the giver of all good gifts and then leave the table with a renewed sense of purpose and power in Jesus. Thanks be to God through His Son our Lord, Jesus Christ.

Prayer: Thank you Father, for the gift of your Son; for His creation of all things and in whose image, I have life, for His work on the cross and in whom I am forgiven, for His gift of the Holy Spirit who brings Joy and Hope to me/us every day. Amen

Devotions for Lord's Supper
Maundy Thursday

The word Maundy taken from a Latin phrase that is translated; "A New Commandment I give to you." John 13:34 The gift of Christ at the supper and the cross is new life through God's love.

Sunday: Exodus 12:1-14 (ESV)

12 *The* L*ORD* *said to Moses and Aaron in the land of Egypt,* ² *"This month shall be for you the beginning of months. It shall be the first month of the year for you.* ³ *Tell all the congregation of Israel that on the tenth day of this month every man shall take a lamb according to their fathers' houses, a lamb for a household.* ⁴ *And if the household is too small for a lamb, then he and his nearest neighbor shall take according to the number of persons; according to what each can eat you shall make your count for the lamb.* ⁵ *Your lamb shall be without blemish, a male a year old. You may take it from the sheep or from the goats,* ⁶ *and you shall keep it until the fourteenth day of this month, when the whole assembly of the congregation of Israel shall kill their lambs at twilight.* [a]7 *"Then they shall take some of the blood and put it on the two doorposts and the lintel of the houses in which they eat it.* ⁸ *They shall eat the flesh that night, roasted on the fire; with unleavened bread and bitter herbs they shall eat it.* ⁹ *Do not eat any of it raw or boiled in water, but roasted, its head with its legs and its inner parts.* ¹⁰ *And you shall let none of it remain until the morning; anything that remains until the morning you shall burn.* ¹¹ *In this manner you shall eat it: with your belt fastened, your sandals on your feet, and your staff in your hand. And you shall eat it in haste. It is the* L*ORD*'s *Passover.* ¹² *For I will pass through the land of Egypt that night, and I will strike all the firstborn in the land of Egypt, both man and beast; and on all the gods of Egypt I will* *execute judgments: I am the LORD. [13] The blood shall be a sign for you, on the houses where you are. And when I see the blood, I will pass over you, and no plague will befall you to destroy you, when I strike the land of Egypt.[14] "This day shall be for you a memorial day, and you shall keep it as a feast to the LORD; throughout your generations, as a statute forever, you shall keep it as a feast.*

Passover as a part of the feast cycle in Israel, was celebrated in three parts. There was first the action of preparation. The Passover was first a promise of God related to His covenant made with Abraham, Isaac and Jacob. The second action was the meal itself. This meal would remind the people of God's action in the past, present and future. The third action was the action of God in response to their faith expressed through the supper and obedience to the blood on the doorposts. God's love is constant from the promise to the fulfillment. Are you prepared, do you see God's action Jesus in the meal, are you ready to celebrate your freedom from sin and death?

Monday: Ezra 6:19-22(ESV)

[19] On the fourteenth day of the first month, the returned exiles kept the Passover. [20] For the priests and the Levites had purified themselves together; all of them were clean. So, they slaughtered the Passover lamb for all the returned exiles, for their fellow priests, and for themselves. [21] It was eaten by the people of Israel who had returned from exile, and also by everyone who had joined them and separated himself from the uncleanness of the peoples of the land to worship the LORD, the God of Israel. [22] And they kept the Feast of Unleavened Bread seven days with joy, for the LORD had made them joyful and had turned the heart of the king of Assyria to them, so that he aided them in the work of the house of God, the God of Israel.

The people have been set free by a foreign king. The stain of another culture that mars and damages beyond repair is removed on going home to Jerusalem. The people rejoice for a week because of God's faithfulness to them. God changed attitudes. God brought freedom. Their response was to separate themselves from unclean actions they had acquired while in exile. We too live in exile from our heavenly home. What behaviors have you acquired you need to abandon to enjoy and celebrate the presence and power of God?

Tuesday: Matthew 26:17-29 (ESV); John 13:31-38 (ESV)

17 Now on the first day of Unleavened Bread the disciples came to Jesus, saying, "Where will you have us prepare for you to eat the Passover?" 18 He said, "Go into the city to a certain man and say to him, 'The Teacher says, My time is at hand. I will keep the Passover at your house with my disciples.'" 19 And the disciples did as Jesus had directed them, and they prepared the Passover. 20 When it was evening, he reclined at table with the twelve.ʲ 21 And as they were eating, he said, "Truly, I say to you, one of you will betray me." 22 And they were very sorrowful and began to say to him one after another, "Is it I, Lord?" 23 He answered, "He who has dipped his hand in the dish with me will betray me. 24 The Son of Man goes as it is written of him, but woe to that man by whom the Son of Man is betrayed! It would have been better for that man if he had not been born." 25 Judas, who would betray him, answered, "Is it I, Rabbi?" He said to him, "You have said so." 26 Now as they were eating, Jesus took bread, and after blessing it broke it and gave it to the disciples, and said, "Take, eat; this is my body." 27 And he took a cup, and when he had given thanks he gave it to them, saying, "Drink of it, all of you, 28 for this is my blood of the[b] covenant, which is poured out for many for the forgiveness of sins. 29 I tell you I will not drink again of this fruit of the vine until that day when I drink it new with you in my Father's kingdom."

The fulfillment of the Passover is in Jesus. Matthew makes that connection clear. John adds to the story. It would help if you had read all of chapter 13. The challenge of John's text is that it reveals the character of God behind the Passover, the supper and the cross. Maundy Thursday reminds us that what Jesus does is born of love. We are to love each other in that same fashion. How loving are you with the people around you?

Wednesday: 1 Corinthians 5:6-8 (ESV)

6 Your boasting is not good. Do you not know that a little leaven leavens the whole lump? 7 Cleanse out the old leaven that you may be a new lump, as you really are unleavened. For Christ, our Passover lamb, has been sacrificed. 8 Let us therefore celebrate the festival, not with the old leaven, the leaven of malice and evil, but with the unleavened bread of sincerity and truth.

Passover had as a part of its ceremony and celebration a rite called Afikomen. A piece of leavened bread was left hidden for children to find. The house was to be rid of all yeast or leaven. It would stain the house. Like sin stains the soul caused by sin, all vestiges of this yeast of leaven need to be removed. In your life as you approach the cross of Christ, His broken body and blood, what sin needs to be searched out and dealt with through confession, repentance and forgiveness?

Thursday: Hebrews 11:24-28 (ESV)

²⁴ By faith Moses, when he was grown up, refused to be called the son of Pharaoh's daughter, ²⁵ choosing rather to be mistreated with the people of God than to enjoy the fleeting pleasures of sin. ²⁶ He considered the reproach of Christ greater wealth than the treasures of Egypt, for he was looking to the reward. ²⁷ By faith he left Egypt, not being afraid of the anger of the king, for he endured as seeing him who is invisible. ²⁸ By faith he kept the Passover and sprinkled the blood, so that the Destroyer of the firstborn might not touch them.

The write of Hebrews goes back to the heroes of the faith, one of which is Moses. As the writer sees it the perfect choice for Moses was God or the culture of Egypt. Moses pushed by God's Spirit and guided by His leading becomes God's witness to the Egyptians, formerly his brothers. Moses expressed faith in two ways; one, through his abandonment of the culture with which he was familiar for another that was alien to him. Then, he was asked to step out in faith and believe that the deliverer would fulfill His promise. Have you divorced yourself from the culture of the world and do you believe that the deliverer will fulfill His promise to you?

Advent Communion Devotions

The Messiah

Monday Isaiah 52:8-10 (ESV) [8] *Listen! Your watchmen lift up their voices; together they shout for joy. When the Lord returns to Zion, they will see it with their own eyes.* [9] *Burst into songs of joy together, you ruins of Jerusalem, for the Lord has comforted his people, he has redeemed Jerusalem.* [10] *The Lord will lay bare his holy arm in the sight of all the nations, and all the ends of the earth will see the salvation of our God.*

When the Lord returns… comfort, redemption and salvation will be ours. Advent anticipates the coming of the Lord. Isaiah brought hope to the exiled and in bondage people with this message. The Advent season looks back to Jesus' birth and looks forward to His coming again for His people. The feast prepared for us is His body and blood for our comfort, redemption, and salvation.

Thought: What are you looking forward to this Advent season?
Tuesday Isaiah 35:3-4(ESV) Strengthen the feeble hands, steady the knees that give way; [4] *say to those with fearful hearts, "Be strong, do not fear; your God will come, he will come with vengeance; with divine retribution he will come to save you."*

It will come as no surprise to all of us that today is not like the good 'old days when being a Christian and celebrating Christmas was exciting and special. In many ways our celebration of the season is in bondage to the demands of the world. How will we rejoice in a foreign land? Be strong and do not fear. Jesus is coming back. Advent is the yearly reminder that no matter what the world is doing to us, what God is doing in us is far greater. And that's the Lord's Supper. What is God in fact doing IN you this year. Come to the table and be filled by the ever-present Son who feeds us and strengthens us.

Prayer: Thank you Father for feeding us at
your table today and each day. Amen

Wednesday Isaiah 35:5-7(ESV) [5] *Then will the eyes of the blind be opened and the ears of the deaf unstopped.* [6] *Then will the lame leap like a deer, and the mute tongue shout for joy. Water will gush forth in the wilderness and streams in the desert.* [7] *The burning sand will become a pool, the thirsty ground bubbling springs. In the haunts where jackals once lay, grass and reeds and papyrus will grow.*

What does Advent and the Lord's table anticipate? Restoration! What Christmas celebrates and Advent anticipates is a newness that comes from God's hand! He announces, "I came that you might have joy in abundance." That joy follows the gifts of forgiveness, grace, and hope. At the table we are reminded of all these things in the body and blood of Jesus Christ. We have the hope of our salvation. We have the recreation of our Spirit. We have the joy of the Good News of Jesus presence.

Activity: Make a list of all the great gifts God has given
you spiritually and then practically or this year.

Thursday Hosea 11:1 1(ESV) *"When Israel was a child, I loved him, and out of Egypt I called my son.*

Here is the table concisely; "For God so loved the World (you) that He gave His only Son." The table is a remembrance of Passover. God called Israel out of Egypt; God calls us out of bondage to self and the world. Then Hosea notes, God calls us. Paul in Ephesians notes, "Before the foundation of the world I chose you." Chosen and called out. The manna of the wilderness is the bread of the table. The cup of the table is the blood of the lamb. Advent reminds us that we have been chosen and called out by God for Him. Be the gift of God to others around you this season.

Prayer: Father, you have equipped and enabled us to
be your presence to your world through your Spirit in
us. Help us to be that this holiday season. Amen

Friday Psalm 51:11 (ESV) *Do not cast me from your*
presence or take your Holy Spirit from me.

This passage is part of David's great prayer of confession after his most
public of sins. The worst punishment that could have afforded him, was
to lose his salvation, lose the power of God, lose his relationship with the
Father. This is the why of confession. Why prepare for the table? Why
confess our sins? To restore our relationship with the Father through the
work of the Son and the presence and power of the Spirit. Advent is God's
reminder to us each year that His Son Jesus cleanses us from all sin. The
table is the symbolic reminder of Jesus presence. Do not push away from
the table this year until you have fed to the full of the Son Jesus.

Prayer and activity: Take a moment to confess your
sins through a prayer of confession tonight.

Saturday Luke 1:41-45 (ESV) [41] *When Elizabeth heard Mary's greeting,*
the baby leaped in her womb, and Elizabeth was filled with the Holy
Spirit. [42] *In a loud voice she exclaimed: "Blessed are you among women*
and blessed is the child you will bear! [43] *But why am I so favored, that*
the mother of my Lord should come to me? [44] *As soon as the sound of your*
greeting reached my ears, the baby in my womb leaped for joy. [45] *Blessed*
is she who has believed that the Lord would fulfill his promises to her!"

The table is the fulfilled promises of God. What promises? Life,
forgiveness, grace, hope, joy, power and strength, mercy …. need we go on?
The table represents to us the person of God in His Son Jesus. His body,
His blood. Why? To fulfill all His covenantal promises to us. Advent is
the fulfilment of God's promises to us in His Son Jesus. Rejoice in the life
God has offered, given and will fulfill completely someday in you!

Activity: Go to or call on the people in your life and be
reconciled to those who you have hurt or who have hurt you.

DEVOTIONS FOR COMMUNION

PASSOVER

Monday - Exodus 12:1-30 (ESV)

The LORD said to Moses and Aaron in the land of Egypt, ² "This month shall be for you the beginning of months. It shall be the first month of the year for you. ³ Tell all the congregation of Israel that on the tenth day of this month every man shall take a lamb according to their fathers' houses, a lamb for a household. ⁴ And if the household is too small for a lamb, then he and his nearest neighbor shall take according to the number of persons; according to what each can eat you shall make your count for the lamb. ⁵ Your lamb shall be without blemish, a male a year old. You may take it from the sheep or from the goats, ⁶ and you shall keep it until the fourteenth day of this month, when the whole assembly of the congregation of Israel shall kill their lambs at twilight. ⁷ "Then they shall take some of the blood and put it on the two doorposts and the lintel of the houses in which they eat it.

This chapter informs us about the central event of Israel's life. The Passover was not a festival or feast; it was an event of God's presence and grace. The event is grounded in God's activity and found fulfillment through the faith of the believer in that promise of God. Now consider the Lord's Supper. Is it not also grounded in God's mighty acts on our behalf? Is it not also fulfilled in the life of the believer as we, through God's gift of faith, are enabled to see Jesus and His presence in our life together as a congregation? The Passover is for all Israel, all those of God's called out ones, who are called by His name. So is communion. List the ways in which God has acted in your life since our last communion celebration.

Tuesday Exodus 19:3-8 (ESV)

³ while Moses went up to God. The Lord *called to him out of the mountain, saying, "Thus you shall say to the house of Jacob, and tell the people of Israel: ⁴ 'You yourselves have seen what I did to the Egyptians, and how I bore you on eagles' wings and brought you to myself. ⁵ Now therefore, if you will indeed obey my voice and keep my covenant, you shall be my treasured possession among all peoples, for all the earth is mine; ⁶ and you shall be to me a kingdom of priests and a holy nation.' These are the words that you shall speak to the people of Israel."*

⁷ So Moses came and called the elders of the people and set before them all these words that the Lord *had commanded him. ⁸ All the people answered together and said, "All that the* Lord *has spoken we will do." And Moses reported the words of the people to the* Lord.

Here we see the consequence of Passover. As with Abraham, "blessed to be a blessing," so here with Israel, set free to bring others to freedom. Here is a grace that ends in a gratitude to God for His gifts. Here is the conclusion of a covenant responsibility. We have been reminded by the bread and cup of communion, of the blood and unleavened bread of the Passover, God's mercy and life. We are reminded that we are redeemed at a price and that our call to follow, our challenge of discipleship is to be God's people for Him and His Kingdom in the world which He has made. When you come to the table can you with the people of Israel say," we will do everything that the Lord has said." What in your life needs to be given over to God before coming to the table?

Wednesday - Leviticus 8: 1-4, 10-13, 30 (ESV)

The Lord *spoke to Moses, saying, ² "Take Aaron and his sons with him, and the garments and the anointing oil and the bull of the sin offering and the two rams and the basket of unleavened bread. ³ And assemble all the congregation at the entrance of the tent of meeting." ⁴ And Moses did as the* Lord *commanded him, and the congregation was assembled at the entrance of the tent of meeting. ¹⁰ Then Moses took the anointing oil and anointed the tabernacle and all that was in it, and consecrated them. ¹¹ And he sprinkled some of it on the altar seven times, and anointed the altar and all its utensils and the basin and its stand, to consecrate them. ¹² And he poured some of the anointing oil on Aaron's head and anointed him to consecrate him. ¹³ And Moses brought Aaron's sons and clothed them with coats and tied sashes around their waists and bound caps on them, as the LORD commanded Moses.*

This chapter looks at the call of God to be priests for the people. It is steeped in the elements of Passover. It has within it the call of God out of bondage and exile into freedom and re-creation. As Priests of God, they are to be separated, Holy, not profane, and dedicated to God and His kingdom and work. Peter reminds us that we are of the same persuasion in 1 Peter 2:5-9 which we will look at Sunday morning. What is the point? You are different. God has declared it to be so and made it so through His Son. We cannot be like the rest of the world but be light within it. When you come to the table on Sunday think about what in your life is like the world and how God has called you out of that place to a new place with Him.

Thursday- Luke 22:1-30 (ESV)

⁷ Then came the day of Unleavened Bread, on which the Passover lamb had to be sacrificed. ⁸ So Jesus[a] sent Peter and John, saying, "Go and prepare the Passover for us, that we may eat it." ⁹ They said to him, "Where will you have us prepare it?" ¹⁰ He said to them, "Behold, when you have entered the city, a man carrying a jar of water will meet you. Follow him into the house that he enters ¹¹ and tell the master of the house, 'The Teacher says to you, Where is the guest room, where I may eat the Passover with my disciples?' ¹² And he will show you a large upper room furnished; prepare it there." ¹³ And they went and found it just as he had told them, and they prepared the Passover.¹⁴ And when the hour came, he reclined at table, and the apostles with him. ¹⁵ And he said to them, "I have earnestly desired to eat this Passover with you before I suffer. ¹⁶ For I tell you I will not eat it[b] until it is fulfilled in the kingdom of God." ¹⁷ And he took a cup, and when he had given thanks he said, "Take this, and divide it among yourselves. ¹⁸ For I tell you that from now on I will not drink of the fruit of the vine until the kingdom of God comes." ¹⁹ And he took bread, and when he had given thanks, he broke it and gave it to them, saying, "This is my body, which is given for you. Do this in remembrance of me." ²⁰ And likewise the cup after they had eaten, saying, "This cup that is poured out for you is the new covenant in my blood.[c] *21 But behold, the hand of him who betrays me is with me on the table. 22 For the Son of Man goes as it has been determined, but woe to that man by whom he is betrayed!" 23 And they began to question one another, which of them it could be who was going to do this.*

I realize this is a long section, but I wanted us to consider the first 6 verses as we thought about Passover and communion. Jesus was not what the elders and learned people of Israel thought a messiah ought to be. Jesus whole life and ministry pointed to a sacrifice that was necessary. Jesus' teaching and works were directed at breaking the bondage to sin and death, much in the same fashion as the exodus Passover. Here in these first 6 verses, we see Jesus and all He has taught and stands for emptied of meaning by the leadership of Israel. He is a nuisance. He is a thorn. He is not like them. Today we have made Jesus in our own image and part of our own culture so much so that we have a challenging time hearing His call to follow Him and lead captives of our culture to Him. When you come to the table can you see in your life how captured by culture you are and how we have attempted to domesticate God in Jesus Christ?

Friday - 1 Corinthians 5: 1-8; 10:1-5 (ESV)

It is actually reported that there is sexual immorality among you, and of a kind that is not tolerated even among pagans, for a man has his father's wife. 2 And you are arrogant! Ought you not rather to mourn? Let him who has done this be removed from among you. 3 For though absent in body, I am present in spirit; and as if present, I have already pronounced judgment on the one who did such a thing. 4 When you are assembled in the name of the Lord Jesus and my spirit is present, with the power of our Lord Jesus, 5 you are to deliver this man to Satan for the destruction of the flesh, so that his spirit may be saved in the day of the Lord.[a]*6 Your boasting is not good. Do you not know that a little leaven leavens the whole lump? 7 Cleanse out the old leaven that you may be a new lump, as you really are unleavened. For Christ, our Passover lamb, has been sacrificed. 8 Let us therefore celebrate the festival, not with the old leaven, the leaven of malice and evil, but with the unleavened bread of sincerity and truth.*

For I do not want you to be unaware, brothers,[a] that our fathers were all under the cloud, and all passed through the sea, 2 and all were baptized into Moses in the cloud and in the sea, 3 and all ate the same spiritual food, 4 and all drank the same spiritual drink. For they drank from the spiritual Rock that followed them, and the Rock was Christ. 5 Nevertheless, with most of them God was not pleased, for they were overthrown[b] in the wilderness.

These two passages are connected by the Lord's supper. In the first passage there is the reference to yeast or leaven and how it damages everything. Passover included as a portion of the ritual, a time for children to search out and remove all the leaven from the place where you lived. Leaven is a symbol for sin. It needs to be rooted out, not because it hurts you but because it hurts everyone. In the Church today, tolerance for sin in all its many forms, has done damage to the body of Christ. "It's always been like this," "That is the way the whole family has been", "You're never going to change them", are part of our vocabulary as a way of explaining our behavior and assuring ourselves of our own righteousness and salvation. It does not make it true. What leaven is in your own life, in your own household and in this body that needs to be cleaned out?

Saturday Hebrews 9:11-22 (ESV)

11 But when Christ appeared as a high priest of the good things that have come, then through the greater and more perfect tent (not made with hands, that is, not of this creation) 12 he entered once for all into the holy places, not by means of the blood of goats and calves but by means of his own blood, thus securing an eternal redemption. 13 For if the blood of goats and bulls, and the sprinkling of defiled persons with the ashes of a heifer, sanctify for the purification of the flesh, 14 how much more will the blood of Christ, who through the eternal Spirit offered himself without blemish to God, purify our conscience from dead works to serve the living God. 15 Therefore he is the mediator of a new covenant, so that those who are called may receive the promised eternal inheritance, since a death has occurred that redeems them from the transgressions committed under the first covenant.[

This text includes several key concepts. Atonement, forgiveness, and covenant are all included here. Exodus was God's atonement for His people. At the price of a lamb, freedom was purchased for an entire nation and all those who believed in them. Forgiveness, the blood of the lamb sprinkled on the altar and the people reminded them that this gift was won for them at the price of a life, and that it was for them in the midst of other sinners. Covenant reminded them that redemption and atonement are never about individuals but about God's grace for a people He has claimed and called out. When we celebrate the Lord's Supper it is a family affair. As much as our world would like us to think it is about us and our salvation alone, it is about the body and God's provision of His Son for us. How are you doing with the other members of the body around you today? What about tomorrow?

Sunday - 1 Peter 2:4-10 (ESV)

4 As you come to him, a living stone rejected by men but in the sight of God chosen and precious, 5 you yourselves like living stones are being built up as a spiritual house, to be a holy priesthood, to offer spiritual sacrifices acceptable to God through Jesus Christ. 6 For it stands in Scripture:

"Behold, I am laying in Zion a stone, a cornerstone chosen and precious, and whoever believes in him will not be put to shame."7 So the honor is for you who believe, but for those who do not believe," The stone that the builders rejected has become the cornerstone,"8 and "A stone of stumbling, and a rock of offense. "They stumble because they disobey the word, as they were destined to do.9 But you are a chosen race, a royal priesthood, a holy nation, a people for his own possession, that you may proclaim the excellencies of him who called you out of darkness into his marvelous light. 10 Once you were not a people, but now you are God's people; once you had not received mercy, but now you have received mercy.

What is it like to be a nobody? Think of adopted children in the old days of orphanages. I know someone like that. Only a first name and not even a given name. No family, no group association that you would like to claim, no home that is yours, and no future. Picture being a ZERO a NOTHING, a NOBODY. Get a good grip on that concept because that is what we call come from before we come to the table this morning. Because of sin and because of rebellion we are nobodies. God's grace extends through the symbols of the table, representing the work of Jesus for us, that we might understand that we are now SOMEBODIES. But we are SOMEBODY only as far as we are by faith tied to Jesus who brings us to the Father. Communion is the family table, a dinner in Jesus' honor thrown by the Father to which we, all those in the family, been invited. This week and year be SOMEBODY, because God says you are in Christ.

First Week of Advent

The Table of the Infants

Monday Genesis 21:1-7 (ESV) Isaac

The LORD visited Sarah as he had said, and the LORD did to Sarah as he had promised. ² And Sarah conceived and bore Abraham a son in his old age at the time of which God had spoken to him. ³ Abraham called the name of his son who was born to him, whom Sarah bore him, Isaac.[a] ⁴ And Abraham circumcised his son Isaac when he was eight days old, as God had commanded him. ⁵ Abraham was a hundred years old when his son Isaac was born to him. ⁶ And Sarah said, "God has made laughter for me; everyone who hears will laugh over me." ⁷ And she said, "Who would have said to Abraham that Sarah would nurse children? Yet I have borne him a son in his old age."

The stories of Abraham and Sarah are filled with lessons for us to learn. Nothing is too big for God, don't laugh at God when He is at work, have faith in God and where He is leading and many more. Today, think about the story of Abraham and Sarah from Isaac's point of view. Talk about putting all your faith in one person!! Isaac is the future not Ishmael. God's kingdom falls on the child of sacrifice, Isaac. Put yourself in Isaac's position. He is a type of Christ, the obedient son who gives himself up in obedience. So, Isaac is set to be sacrificed in obedience to God's command. Are we willing to give ourselves up in obedience to God's command? Ponder that this week as we look at the Lord's supper from the Table of the Infants.

Prayer: Help us Father, to be the kind of people who willingly give ourselves up for God and His Kingdom. Amen

Tuesday Genesis 25:21-26 (ESV) Jacob

And Isaac prayed to the LORD for his wife, because she was barren. And the LORD granted his prayer, and Rebekah his wife conceived. ²² The children struggled together within her, and she said, "If it is thus, why is this happening to me?" So she went to inquire of the LORD. ²³ And the LORD said to her,

"Two nations are in your womb,
and two peoples from within you shall be divided;
the one shall be stronger than the other,
the older shall serve the younger."

²⁴ When her days to give birth were completed, behold, there were twins in her womb. ²⁵ The first came out red, all his body like a hairy cloak, so they called his name Esau. ²⁶ Afterward his brother came out with his hand holding Esau's heel, so his name was called Jacob. Isaac was sixty years old when she bore them.

"Two nations are in your womb." One will be a diligent worker, the other a mama's boy, one will be an honest though uncommitted son, the other a sneak and a liar. One is older by minutes, the other younger by the same amount. Who does God choose? "Jacob, have I loved, Esau have I hated." Those words are among the most difficult to understand in the Bible. These twins, born of a woman who has to this point been barren like Sarah, have the seed of humanity shot through them. They are me! Who does God choose for His work? God chooses whom He chooses and it is His sovereign will. Today as you think about the Table of Infants, remember that we are here, not because we chose to be but because God chose us to be. The challenge is to be committed and faithful to that call. The call of God is confirmed at the table. The table represents the ultimate commitment.

Ponder: Look back to your call from God and your profession. Are you as committed and obedient today as you were then? What do you need to do to get back to that point?

Wednesday Exodus 2:1-10 (ESV) Moses

Now a man from the house of Levi went and took as his wife a Levite woman. ² The woman conceived and bore a son, and when she saw that he was a fine child, she hid him three months. ³ When she could hide him no longer, she took for him a basket made of bulrushes⁽ᵃ⁾ and daubed it with bitumen and pitch. She put the child in it and placed it among the reeds by the river bank. ⁴ And his sister stood at a distance to know what would be done to him. ⁵ Now the daughter of Pharaoh came down to bathe at the river, while her young women walked beside the river. She saw the basket among the reeds and sent her servant woman, and she took it. ⁶ When she opened it, she saw the child, and behold, the baby was crying. She took pity on him and said, "This is one of the Hebrews' children." ⁷ Then his sister said to Pharaoh's daughter, "Shall I go and call you a nurse from the Hebrew women to nurse the child for you?" ⁸ And Pharaoh's daughter said to her, "Go." So the girl went and called the child's mother. ⁹ And Pharaoh's daughter said to her, "Take this child away and nurse him for me, and I will give you your wages." So the woman took the child and nursed him. ¹⁰ When the child grew older, she brought him to Pharaoh's daughter, and he became her son. She named him Moses, "Because," she said, "I drew him out of the water.

Moses is a remarkable story about adoption. First, Pharaoh's daughter adopts Moses. Then God is adopting Moses to lead His family to freedom. Finally, God's people adopt Moses back into their family where he belonged all along. Moses' life is a lot like ours. Living a lie, we are created in God's image are adopted by the world and become like it rather than becoming like Him. Then, God calls and adopts us as His own and we no longer live a lie but life. Then, the Church becomes our mother, and we have a new family. We all need to be adopted by God and by the Church to truly live. Moses' life reminds us that left alone we will die. But once adopted by God we live and have joy. When you come to the table, remember your adoption by God and the church and have the joy of your salvation!

*Activity: **What did you receive when you were adopted by God by grace and faith to believe, as His child? Make a list of all the great gifts God has given.***

Thursday 1 Samuel 3:1-10 (ESV) Samuel

Now the boy Samuel was ministering to the Lord in the presence of Eli. And the word of the Lord was rare in those days; there was no frequent vision.² At that time Eli, whose eyesight had begun to grow dim so that he could not see, was lying down in his own place. ³ The lamp of God had not yet gone out, and Samuel was lying down in the temple of the LORD, where the ark of God was.⁴ Then the LORD called Samuel, and he said, "Here I am!"⁵ and ran to Eli and said, "Here I am, for you called me." But he said, "I did not call; lie down again." So he went and lay down.⁶ And the LORD called again, "Samuel!" and Samuel arose and went to Eli and said, "Here I am, for you called me." But he said, "I did not call, my son; lie down again." ⁷ Now Samuel did not yet know the LORD, and the word of the LORD had not yet been revealed to him.⁸ And the LORD called Samuel again the third time. And he arose and went to Eli and said, "Here I am, for you called me." Then Eli perceived that the LORD was calling the boy. ⁹ Therefore Eli said to Samuel, "Go, lie down, and if he calls you, you shall say, 'Speak, LORD, for your servant hears.'" So Samuel went and lay down in his place.¹⁰ And the LORD came and stood, calling as at other times, "Samuel! Samuel!" And Samuel said, "Speak, for your servant hears."

We've talked about getting called and answering in obedience. We have talked about commitment and faithfulness. Yesterday we talked about adoption. Here we see all three illustrated in the life of Samuel. Given over by his mother because of a promise, Samuel is adopted by Eli into his family. He is obedient to this call even though he is taken from his mother. Samuel hears God's voice and answers the call. When God calls us are we like Samuel. Do we answer not only, "here I am," but then follow through on that call to be what God calls us to be and do what God calls us to do. Coming to the Table of Infants, we are reminded that we are called of God not just for the calling's sake but for a purpose for Him and His kingdom. Did you hear the call this week of the infants of Advent and the nativity, and will you answer that call?

Prayer: Father in heaven, help me to not only hear your voice like Samuel but stand firm and resolute to answer that call that you give. Amen

Friday Luke 1:57-66 (ESV) John the Baptist

⁵⁷ Now the time came for Elizabeth to give birth, and she bore a son. ⁵⁸ And her neighbors and relatives heard that the Lord had shown great mercy to her, and they rejoiced with her. ⁵⁹ And on the eighth day they came to circumcise the child. And they would have called him Zechariah after his father, ⁶⁰*but his mother answered, "No; he shall be called John." ⁶¹And they said to her, "None of your relatives is called by this name." ⁶² And they made signs to his father, inquiring what he wanted him to be called. ⁶³ And he asked for a writing tablet and wrote, "His name is John." And they all wondered. ⁶⁴ And immediately his mouth was opened and his tongue loosed, and he spoke, blessing God. ⁶⁵ And fear came on all their neighbors. And all these things were talked about through all the hill country of Judea, ⁶⁶ and all who heard them laid them up in their hearts, saying, "What then will this child be?"*

I love this story for several reasons, but I want to focus on one for today. The name, John! The Greek form of this name is Ioanne and it means "God's gracious gift." Our daughter has the feminine form of that name, Yvana. John was God's gracious gift not only to his parents but to all humanity. He is the prophesied forerunner for Jesus. He is the prophet who sets the stage for the good news of Jesus Christ to come into the world. Jesus Christ, as the living Word, is the platform God uses for the gospel to be present to and accepted by the world. John is amazing. He calls the people to repent. He calls the people back to God. He is God's gift. Of course, this gift points to the other that is to come, Jesus. As you come to the table Sunday, remember, God's gracious gift to you. It is life and wholeness. John's message points us in the right direction, repent or turn from your sin and back to God and be baptized. As you prepare, repent and believe the good news of God given to you in the person of Jesus Christ.

Ponder: When you receive a gift what do you do with it? Have you ever just left a gift unopened and then re-gifted it to someone else? How often do we do that we Jesus?

Saturday Luke 2:1-7 (ESV) Jesus the Christ

In those days a decree went out from Caesar Augustus that all the world should be registered. ² This was the first registration when[a] Quirinius was governor of Syria. ³ And all went to be registered, each to his own town. ⁴ And Joseph also went up from Galilee, from the town of Nazareth, to Judea, to the city of David, which is called Bethlehem, because he was of the house and lineage of David, ⁵ to be registered with Mary, his betrothed,[b] who was with child. ⁶ And while they were there, the time came for her to give birth. ⁷ And she gave birth to her firstborn son and wrapped him in swaddling cloths and laid him in a manger, because there was no place for them in the inn.

Here is the culmination of The Table of Infants that point to the sacrifice of God for us. Jesus is born to die. Jesus is born to set the world free. Jesus is born to bear the sins of the world from time immemorial. Jesus, the one who saves His people from their sins, will lie before us tomorrow in the form of the bread and the cup. When the infant, Jesus, is acknowledged by the wise men, they are found bringing the symbols of Jesus work: prophet, priest, and King. Mark 1:15 is the conclusion of the Gospel of Mark's opening section. The time has come. The kingdom is near. Repent and believe the good news. As you come to the table tomorrow, know these things: The time is now. The kingdom is near. Now do these things: Repent, turn from your sin and believe the good news of God in Jesus.

Activity: What do you need to repent of and give over to God? Make a list and pray for it. Do you have a relationship with Jesus Christ that is dynamic and ail?

Communion Devotions

The Light of the World

There is no life without light. There is no way to find your way without light. There is no hope without light (the light at the end of the tunnel). Jesus is the light of the World.

Monday - *Genesis 1:3-5(ESV)* **3 And God said, "Let there be light," and there was light. 4 God saw that the light was good, and he separated the light from the darkness. 5 God called the light "day," and the darkness he called "night."*

Did you ever wonder why the first thing God created was light? Not only is this consistent with physical reality, (there is no life without life so there could be no animals, plants, or insects) but it is also a spiritual reality. In the darkness (the Hebrew says, chaos, disorder, and emptiness of time), there enters this Godly light. It provides the warmth and energy for life. It provides the hope of new tomorrows. Jesus is that light of the world. Communion reminds us Jesus as the light of the world gives life to those who follow Him and in whom Jesus dwells. The Bread and the Cup are the signs of God's indwelling with us.

Activity: try taking away light from one of your plants over the course of this week and see how it looks at the end of the week. How much do we need the light?

Tuesday - *Psalm 27:1(ESV)* *The Lord is my light and my salvation— whom shall I fear? The Lord is the stronghold of my life— of whom shall I be afraid?*

The Lord (Yahweh, the great I am, I was, I have been, and I will be forever), is my light and my salvation. The Lord is my salvation! Ponder that for a moment. What does it mean to you to have life by light? Think about a ship in a storm headed for who knows what. Suddenly a light pierces the darkness and warns you that the rocks are near, and you are about to sink. The light is both a warning and a savior. It reminds us that we cannot do this thing called the journey of life on our own. We need someone to guide us through the storms and help save us when the rocks of life threaten to destroy us. Communion is that guiding light. Jesus as the light of the world guides us to life, hope and joy.

Prayer: Dear Lord, guide us by the light of your Son Jesus Christ that we might find safety and shelter in the harbor of your love. Amen

Wednesday – *Isaiah 49:6(ESV)* *he says: "It is too small a thing for you to be my servant to restore the tribes of Jacob and bring back those of Israel I have kept. I will also make you a light for the Gentiles, that my salvation may reach to the ends of the earth."*

Salvation is NEVER an exclusively self-oriented deal. Here in Isaiah, the prophet notes that God's salvation comes with a condition. It is not that salvation is conditional. It is that salvation that is truly from God prompts a gracious and spontaneous response. Israel to reflect their saved status would become God's servant. As such they would bring the message of God's grace and salvation to the gentiles. It is in that sense that Israel is the light of the world or at least they were supposed to be the light of the world. The Lord's Table reminds us that it is there we have our needs met by Jesus, while at the same time we rejoice, the overflow of God's love to those around us. At the table, this year at Christmas, think about not just getting a gift of light but being that gift of light to others.

Response: Who can you share the light of salvation with this year? Give the greatest gift of all!

Thursday – John 1:4-5 (ESV) In *him was life, and that life was the light of all mankind. 5 The light shines in the darkness, and the darkness has not overcome it.*

John the Baptist is a model for each of us. He wields the light like a lantern, a beacon. John is not the light. Jesus is the light. But John points to that light so that others might understand something clearly at last through Him and therefore know Him. The same thing happens every time we come to the table. We are not the light of God, but that light shines through us. You know how people say, "you are what you eat." Well, having come to the table to meet Jesus, as He becomes one with us in the meal, we become what we eat. This is a good thing! Then, when people see us, they will indeed see Jesus. If Christmas is in part about a star that drew people to Jesus to worship, so we allow that light to shine through us so that others may see Him. It starts at the table!

Prayer: Father in heaven, may we in having been with Jesus, shine that light of your love to the world around us.

Friday – Romans 2:19-21(ESV) *if you are convinced that you are a guide for the blind, a light for those who are in the dark, 20 an instructor of the foolish, a teacher of little children, because you have in the law the embodiment of knowledge and truth— 21 you, then, who teach others, do you not teach yourself?*

To walk by the law is darkness. It only leads to self-congratulatory work. It is what transpired for Israel with the sacrificial system they followed. What you get is, "I followed the law. If and when I did not, I followed the law of the sacrifice. I am good!" This is not what God had intended. Exodus 20 makes it clear that gratitude should have been the response to God's passing over His people. The same can be said of us today about our relationship to the Father through the sacrifice of the Son. The Lord's table, called the Eucharist, means thanks be to God. Our response to God in the supper ought to be the same as Israel's was supposed to be, thanksgiving. When we come to the table, we are a light of gratitude to God for the gift of salvation and grace that shines through us. May you find or rediscover this gift of God at His table this Sunday.

Activity: For what are you grateful to God this week and this year?

Saturday - Colossians 1:12-14 (ESV) *"and giving joyful thanks to the Father, who has qualified you to share in the inheritance of his holy people in the kingdom of light. 13 For he has rescued us from the dominion of darkness and brought us into the kingdom of the Son he loves, 14 in whom we have redemption, the forgiveness of sins."*

This text takes us back to the beginning of our week and scripture. This is a part of Paul's creation narrative. The passage combines the twin ideas of giving thanks to God (eucharist; also, the name for the Lord's Supper) and the creation of light as the first element of that creation. Paul says that it is of and through Jesus Christ, the only begotten Son of the Father, that we are rescued from the dominion of darkness. The same idea is in Genesis 1:1-3. Out of the chaos of the world, God has rescued us and given us life. Thanks be to God for that rescue. Thanks be to God for that hope. Thanks be to God for that life. The Lord's table on the first Sunday of Advent reminds us that through Jesus all things that have been created were made through Him, who is the Word, and that in Jesus we have the hope of forgiveness and life and by Jesus we will be rescued from death and destruction. This truth is the foundation of Advent, Christmas and the story of God, scripture! Come to the table out of the darkness of the world and walk into the light of life in Jesus Christ.

Prayer: Thank you heavenly Father for your Son Jesus and the life and light we have been given through Him. Bless us tomorrow at your table as we say thanks for that life and light. Amen

Communion Devotions

From the Gray Psalter Liturgy

Monday - 1 Cor. 11:27-28 (ESV)

²⁷ Whoever, therefore, eats the bread or drinks the cup of the Lord in an unworthy manner will be guilty concerning the body and blood of the Lord. ²⁸ Let a person examine himself, then, and so eat of the bread and drink of the cup.

Examine yourself! What this means is a test to determine if something is genuine. In this case what Paul is talking about is one is faith/works in the fashion that James talks about faith and works. Examine your own life this week as you approach the table, in what do you have faith and how that faith is expressed. The Lord's Supper is about the body of Christ. That being the case, we are to care for, tend to build up the body of Christ to the glory of God. If in any way we have not done that, we are to repent and seek forgiveness. Then having examined ourselves we can come to the table and restore that sense of our being attached to and a member of the body of Christ.

ACTIVITY: *Spend time today considering and examining yourself to see how your faith/works are doing.*

Tuesday - 1 Cor. 10:17 (ESV)

¹⁷ Because there is one bread, we who are many are one body, for we all partake of the one bread.

As we gather next Sunday, we will be one body. Although throughout this week, in individual homes throughout the southland area we have gathered as individual families, we are now engaged together as one great family of God. Though individually, your family is special and unique, collectively, like the Church, we are magnified to be even better and more special to the praise of His glory. It is like a single grain of wheat that goes into bread. A miracle in its own right and nutritious, when added together with others it is quite special. It becomes a loaf of incredible value to people. It is the staff of life. So, this coming Sunday as you come together with all of God's people, realize how unique and special you are but also realize how much more special we are as a family of God, the one loaf in Christ for this community.

Prayer: Father in heaven, help us as a family recognize our uniqueness but also recognize our value together as a family made up by you, for you, for this community. AMEN

Wednesday -Matthew 11:28-29 (ESV)

²⁸ Come to me, all who labor and are heavy laden, and I will give you rest. ²⁹ Take my yoke upon you, and learn from me, for I am gentle and lowly in heart, and you will find rest for your souls.

What is the point of the Lord's Supper if it is not just a part of the worship experience, or it's not just a memorial feast? According to Jesus in this passage, the point of the supper is for Him to carry our burdens and relieve our weariness at living life. The point is for us to begin to realize the full depth and measure of the work of Jesus in the forgiveness of sins, (our burdens) and embrace us in the fragility of life, (weariness). The Lord's Supper should remind us that in Jesus we have all that we need as symbolized by the bread and the cup. It is Jesus Himself; we take to ourselves. When we do this, we are filled to the full with the life and power, the grace and hope of God Himself who has made us. When you come to the table, leave behind all your burdens and be filled with the life of God.

ACTIVITY: *This week spend some time thinking about your sins; those things you have done that separate you from others. Make a list of those things and give them to God.*

Thursday - Matthew 5:6 (ESV)

⁶ "Blessed are those who hunger and thirst for righteousness, for they shall be satisfied.

We have talked about this recently. What does it mean to hunger after something? Have you ever experienced true hunger? While I have been hungry just for food, there have been more times in my life where I have hungered for a certain kind of food, you know, "I could sure go for an in-n-out burger right now!" sort of thing. My question for all of us this week is, do you hunger for more of Jesus and of His kingdom? Do we hunger for the fullness of God? Spiritually, are you hungry or are you satisfied? When we come to the Lord's Table, it should be to be filled with the full promise of God and of His Spirit. How will you come to the table this week? Will you come full of what you currently have spiritually, full of yourself, full of the world around you or will you come hungering and thirsting for righteousness?

Prayer: Father in heaven, help me/us this week to want more of you every day so that as I/we come to the table, I desire to be filled to the full with your grace and power. Amen

Friday - Revelation 1:5-6

⁵ and from Jesus Christ the faithful witness, the firstborn of the dead, and the ruler of kings on earth. To him who loves us and has freed us from our sins by his blood ⁶ and made us a kingdom, priests to his God and Father, to him be glory and dominion forever and ever. Amen.

"To Him who loved us and freed us from our sins by His blood and has made us to be a kingdom and priests to serve His God and Father- To God be the glory and power for ever and ever." To God be the glory great things He has done; this is our vision statement. Everything to the glory of God. Whatever we are and whatever we do, all to the glory of God. The challenge in communion is not in the church during worship but the living out daily this glory of God wherever we are and whatever we do. All to the glory of God. Jesus' death was to the glory of God. His resurrection was to the glory of God. Our forgiveness and inclusion in the kingdom are to the glory of God. When you come to the table this Sunday, remember that the reason you are there is because of the glory of God revealed in Jesus and then when you leave on Sunday remember that you live because of the glory of God given to you in Jesus.

Prayer: Father in heaven, help us to live so that your glory shines from us wherever we go and whatever we do. In Jesus name, Amen.

Saturday - Psalm 103:1-4

Bless the LORD, O my soul, and all that is within me, bless his holy name! *² Bless the LORD, O my soul, and forget not all his benefits, ³ who forgives all your iniquity, who heals all your diseases, ⁴ who redeems your life from the pit, who crowns you with steadfast love and mercy,*

The word used here for blessing is the same word used in Genesis 1:28. The word is Barakah, to bless. It means to bow down before, to worship and adore. The word reflects God's incredible joy at what He has created in humanity. In the Lord's Supper it reflects the Lord's servants' attitude and heart at what He has done on the cross and empty tomb. Here is Psalm 103 we stand between those two blessings of God. We bless the Lord (which is an imperative), because of both works of God. We stand between creation and recreation that only God can do. As you come to the table tomorrow, remember who made you, who called you, who saved you and who filled you. This is God's blessing to us in Communion!

Prayer: Dear Jesus, thank you for the work you have done for us. Father in Heaven, thank you for claiming us. Holy Spirit, thank you for filling us with the power of God bought and paid for by the work of the triune God. Amen

Behold; I Make All Things New!

Devotions for a New Year

Monday: **Ezekiel 40:1**

> *In the twenty-fifth year of our exile, at the beginning of the*
> *year, on the tenth day of the month, in the fourteenth year*
> *after the city was struck down, on that very day, the hand of*
> *the L*ORD *was upon me, and he brought me to the city*

Most people like new over old. Would you rather have a new car or an old, used car? In the Hebrew calendar, the new year followed the day of atonement closely. This is not a coincidence or an accident. There is something about becoming new. It's one of the most fervent longings of humanity. We want new starts, new school years with new classes, a new job. New holds out the endless possibilities of hope. Jesus says we are a new creation. Through our participation in confession, assurance and in the body of Christ, communion, we become new through God's work in the Spirit and at the table.

Activity: What areas of your life need to be made over and renewed today? Make a list and commit it to God in prayer.

Tuesday   **Psalm 19:7-11**

> *The law of the L*ORD *is perfect, reviving the soul;*
> *the testimony of the L*ORD *is sure,*
> *making wise the simple;* [8] *the precepts of the L*ORD *are right,*
> *rejoicing the heart; the commandment of the L*ORD *is pure,*
> *enlightening the eyes;* [9] *the fear of the L*ORD *is clean,*

*enduring forever; the rules of the L*ORD *are true, and righteous altogether.*
¹⁰ More to be desired are they than gold, even much fine gold; sweeter
also than honey and drippings of the honeycomb. ¹¹ Moreover, by them
is your servant warned; in keeping them there is great reward.

One of the texts that the people of God read during Rosh Hashanah (the new years' service in Israel) was Psalm 19. Part of starting over was coming to grips with the command of God to obey and follow Him. If the believer/ Israelite/chosen one of God would follow the law, he would have a renewed life, have joy be wise, finally get life that endures forever. In truth, to start over and follow the Word and will of God would change a person's life. Things are much simpler now. We are born again in Jesus (renewed), we are recreated in Christ (restored), and we are renewed by the Spirit. This is symbolized by what we do at the Lord's table. Be new by following Jesus!

Thought: In what ways in your life can you follow the Word and Will of God better?

Wednesday   Genesis 22:13-14

¹³ And Abraham lifted up his eyes and looked, and behold, behind him
was a ram, caught in a thicket by his horns. And Abraham went and
took the ram and offered it up as a burnt offering instead of his son. ¹⁴
*So Abraham called the name of that place, "The L*ORD *will provide"; as*
*it is said to this day, "On the mount of the L*ORD *it shall be provided."*

This passage used at this time of year reflects a new lease on life. Isaac, the first born and only son, was slated to be the sacrifice to God for His Blessing of Abraham. Isaac says earlier in this passage, "where is the sacrifice?" Abraham replies, "God will provide!" Indeed, God provides something new. Instead of our making the effort, our providing, God does all the work, and He provides. The price for our sin and depravity is His only begotten Son. The Supper in which we take part gives us this fresh start in life.

Prayer: Thank you Yahweh Jireh (God the provider) for providing
for my sins and my life through your Son Jesus Christ. Amen

Thursday   Exodus 19:16-19

*¹⁶ On the morning of the third day there were thunders and lightnings and a thick cloud on the mountain and a very loud trumpet blast, so that all the people in the camp trembled. ¹⁷ Then Moses brought the people out of the camp to meet God, and they took their stand at the foot of the mountain. ¹⁸ Now Mount Sinai was wrapped in smoke because the L*ORD *had descended on it in fire. The smoke of it went up like the smoke of a kiln, and the whole mountain trembled greatly. ¹⁹ And as the sound of the trumpet grew louder and louder, Moses spoke, and God answered him in thunder.*

If seeing is believing, this passage exemplifies it. Yahweh (God) has talked to Moses and told him to remind the people of what He has done for them (pass over of the angel of death and passage through the red sea to new life). Now the people of God get to "see" this great God who is personal and has set them free. In the bread and cup, we too see the God who has set us free. We see Him in all His shame and humiliation and in all His resurrected glory. When you come to the table renew your relationship with this great personal God who has set you free from sin and death.

Activity: What have you seen God do for you this past year?

Friday   Romans 13:11-14

¹¹ Besides this you know the time, that the hour has come for you to wake from sleep. For salvation is nearer to us now than when we first believed. ¹² The night is far gone; the day is at hand. So then let us cast off the works of darkness and put on the armor of light. ¹³ Let us walk properly as in the daytime, not in orgies and drunkenness, not in sexual immorality and sensuality, not in quarreling and jealousy. ¹⁴ But put on the Lord Jesus Christ, and make no provision for the flesh, to gratify its desires.

Let us not talk about the past. I do not want to know how long ago you professed your faith. Let us talk about the present. We all need to wake up to the twin realities of our sin and depravity and that of the world around us and the second reality of God's grace, love, and salvation. The night is over. It is time to wake up to the newness of the Spirit and the life that God gives. Today after we pray, put what is past behind and press on to the upward call of God in a renewed relationship with Jesus Christ!

Prayer: Father in heaven, help us to wake up to a new reality today. Help us to live out the reality of the resurrected Jesus living in our life. In your name, Amen.

Saturday　　Ephesians 5:13-16

13 But when anything is exposed by the light, it becomes visible, 14 for anything that becomes visible is light. Therefore it says,

"Awake, O sleeper,
and arise from the dead,
and Christ will shine on you."

15 Look carefully then how you walk, not as unwise but as wise, 16 making the best use of the time, because the days are evil.

A new day is dawning. The light has come. The darkness of night, including the dark night of the soul, will be driven away. We have been doing a series about the dark places of the soul. Think about waking up to a new day where the darkness is driven away not just in that spiritual sense of the light of Christ, but more practically as Jesus drives the darkness of depression, bitterness, anger, mistakes away. Think about what living a new life lived fully in the light of God's grace and love will look like.

When you come to the table tomorrow, come in the light, fully illumined by God's grace and then be a light to all those who you meet!

Thought: "Light, even though it passes through pollution is not polluted." St. Augustine And I saw that there was an ocean of darkness and death; but an infinite ocean of light and love flowed over the ocean of darkness; and in that I saw the infinite love of God.

Devotions for Communion
Acceptance and Welcome

You're Welcome!

Monday 2 Kings 4:8-10

⁸ One day Elisha went on to Shunem, where a wealthy woman lived, who urged him to eat some food. So whenever he passed that way, he would turn in there to eat food. ⁹ And she said to her husband, "Behold now, I know that this is a holy man of God who is continually passing our way. ¹⁰ Let us make a small room on the roof with walls and put there for him a bed, a table, a chair, and a lamp, so that whenever he comes to us, he can go in there."

Doing God's will and caring for others provokes a welcome. This story of the Shunammite woman and her on-going relationship with Elisha provides a great parable for how God works with us. God provides for us. God raises us from the dead. God feeds us. All He requires is a welcome. Are we welcoming of God into our lives, and do we feel welcomed to God at His table? Are we accepting and giving at this table in the same fashion God has been for us? Do you feel welcome here? This table is for those who have misplaced worship as self-glorifying or satisfying, for those who have sought to be served rather than serve others and for those who have been redeemed from death to life. You're Welcome!!!

Prayer: Heavenly Father, may we find a warm welcome at your table, and may we be as good a host to others as you have been for us. Amen

Tuesday Isaiah 55:1-2

"Come, everyone who thirsts, come to the waters; and he who has no money, come, buy, and eat!

Come, buy wine and milk without money and without price. ² Why do you spend your money for that which is not bread, and your labor for that which does not satisfy? Listen diligently to me, and eat what is good, and delight yourselves in rich food.

God's offer is wide open. We come from a tradition that believes strongly in God's call and what we call Election. This passage broadens that understanding. God offers to all who are thirsty and hungry an opportunity for the infilling and satisfaction of the good things of God at no cost to us. His welcome is to ALL who are thirsty and hungry. Granted, the message of the prophet is written to the people of God, Israel, but it does say all. God's welcome is gracious to all who bear His image. Jesus reinforces this with his parable about the wedding feast and the invitation that extends beyond those first invited. So how about it? Do you feel welcome and how would you feel about welcoming others to God's table of salvation for which He has already paid?

Application: When someone offers to buy you dinner do you decline? What if we offered those around us a chance to dine with God and us next week? Are they welcome?

Wednesday Luke 14:8-11

⁸ *"When you are invited by someone to a wedding feast, do not sit down in a place of honor, lest someone more distinguished than you be invited by him, ⁹ and he who invited you both will come and say to you, 'Give your place to this person,' and then you will begin with shame to take the lowest place. ¹⁰ But when you are invited, go and sit in the lowest place, so that when your host comes he may say to you, 'Friend, move up higher.' Then you will be honored in the presence of all who sit at table with you. ¹¹ For everyone who exalts himself will be humbled, and he who humbles himself will be exalted."*

This parable is about those who assume too much about their welcome to the feast and the table. Assuming since they have been invited by the host, they must be the most important ones there, they take the place of honor. Only the host can determine that. Only the host can determine if your invitation is valid, and you even have a place. The Host is God. The invitation has gone out through Jesus Christ. The invitation has gone out this week. It has gone out to you and through you to others. How welcoming are we and are we so grateful to God that we enter and say thanks be to God, (Eucharist) to which He replies, You're Welcome.

Thought: How welcome do you feel when you come before the table of the Lord despite your sin or lifestyle? Have you extended that invitation and welcome to others despite their sin or lifestyle?

Thursday Hebrews 13:2

² *Do not neglect to show hospitality to strangers, for thereby some have entertained angels unawares.*

Met any strangers lately? Met anyone strange lately? That last question is not an attempt to be funny. Jesus made a habit of being with the strange people. The demon possessed man in the cemetery, the prostitute, the gentile; all those considered strangers and outsiders. He was hung on a cross between the two of them, thieves and murderers. Jesus welcomed them all. It's the same welcome He extends to us at the table. I'm guessing you know some strange people. What is your relationship with them like? Would you invite them to the table and share a meal with them? As you consider the table of the Lord this week, consider your relationship with the stranger. Remember, you were a stranger to the Lord before you became family. Invite the stranger; adopt them the way God did you and make them family!

Consider: Who could you invite to be a part of God's family here? Let us expand our welcome and embrace others as part of God's family!

Friday Revelation 22:17

¹⁷ *The Spirit and the Bride say, "Come." And let the one who hears say, "Come." And let the one who is thirsty come; let the one who desires take the water of life without price.*

In this last chapter of the last book of the bible, God once again calls all those created in His image to come. Come to the table. Come to the water of life. The welcome of God is granted to ALL. I can remember our welcomes in all our Churches we have served. In times past, we were greeted by God's people and frequently with a food shower. In that regard, it is not just one meal but a feast for days or weeks. In Iowa, we got enough meat to last for months. This is like the manna and quail in the wilderness. God has invited to be served by Himself through the host, Jesus. The meal is prepared. You were welcome. You have conversed with God. Now, God can feed us. ALL are welcome.

Prayer: Thank you Father for the meal which you have prepared and to which you have invited us. May we be as much a blessing to others as you have blessed us, through Jesus Christ our Lord, Amen.

Saturday 2 Corinthians 6:2

²For he says "In a favorable time I listened to you, and in a day of salvation I have helped you. "Behold, now is the favorable time; behold, now is the day of salvation.

This is the time of God's favor. The invitation from God to come to the table, has been offered. Note that the invitation is to salvation and life. To be grateful at the table is to celebrate the Eucharist (the thanksgiving meal) deeply and personally, intensely and passionately. God's greeting, welcome and relationship is accompanied not by a requirement but with a gift. The gift of God is His Son which is life. Like with Israel in Egypt and Passover, this gift of God is accompanied by a sacrifice that sets us free. "You are welcome here" comes after our profound thanks be to God through our Lord Jesus Christ. When you come tomorrow know that God's "You're welcome" is preceded by our own sense of gratitude and thanks for His Son and our salvation.

Thought: For what are you thankful that God has given besides and on top of your salvation? For example: your life, hope, power, and so on.

Good Friday Devotions and Liturgy - Sacrifice

Tonight, for communion you will need to do several things: Have your sins written down on a separate slip of paper (either the one provided or one of your own), you are offering for God handy, and have read these directions. Tonight, the elders are asking you to come forward for communion. For those of you who are unable or unwilling to do so, communion will be served to you where you are sitting. While you are seated or waiting to come forward in line, please sing the songs that you will see on the screen. For those that come forward we ask that you form two lines in the center aisle. When you come to the center of the Church, place your paper with your sins written on it on one of the nails of the cross. Please take communion from the Pastor and elder who are on your side of the aisle. When you receive the bread and cup, partake of both when they are given you. As you are going to the side aisle to take your original seat, please place your offering on the plate that is at the end of the front aisle or in the hand of a deacon.

__Preparatory Exhortation:__ The concept of self-sacrifice is foreign to us today. This is especially true spiritually. We have been trained for self-reliance. We are trained for independence. Coming from a covenantal Church background the challenge to us then is to think not in terms of self but others, not in terms of getting our own but giving our all. Jesus' sacrifice is the perfect example of this. The story of Abraham and Isaac and Abraham's willingness to sacrifice his only son, provide the backdrop story for Jesus' work on the cross. Tonight, as you approach the cross, think about Jesus as that only Son, like Isaac. Dear to the Father, yet the Father gives Him up. Someone has died that you might live. Now come to the cross and the table and have fellowship with the loving Father who makes it all possible through His sacrificial Son.

Formulary: *"On the night He was betrayed Jesus took bread and after He had given thanks and blessed it, He broke it and said, this is my body which is broken for you. Take eat. After they had supped Jesus took the cup and said, this is the new covenant in my blood shed for you for the forgiveness of sins."* Take and drink. (Matthew 26:26,27 ESV) That Thursday night Jesus served the disciples in preparation for Passover and in Passover. The sacrifice had not yet been made but in a sense had already been made. God had become flesh, had become like us so that we might have hope and new life. The sacrifice was already made at the foundation of creation when God made the Universe and sacrificed by giving of Himself in the creation of humanity; we are made in His image. God blesses us and we in turn, in receiving that blessing, share in God's joy and power. At the cross the power of love overturns sin and hatred, the power of sacrifice overturns death and hell.

Prayer and Lord's Prayer: No God can compare with you, O Lord; your works are awesome. Nations bow before you. They glorify your name. Your greatness penetrates each moment of our day. Through the night you care for us. As the day dawns your splendor fills the heavens. Aw we arise and give you glory; you empower us to serve you in all we do. Not a breath passes our lips that we do not know of your presence. Now we enter the gates of your temple to sing to you, our praises. We pray this in the name of our Lord Jesus Christ who taught His disciples to pray....

Invitation All those who are sincerely sorry for their sins, who have confessed the name of Jesus and who are confessing members of an evangelical church are welcome to this table. The table falls in the shadow of the cross. Let the sacrifice of Jesus fall in your life as well as you dine with Him.

Distribution of the elements: (Please follow the instructions you will find at the top of this page after the invitation to the table that follows) The bread which we break is to us the body of Christ and the cup of blessing is to us the blood of Christ. You are welcome at the table.

Prayer of thanksgiving: What shall we render to the Lord for all His kindness shown? Our feet shall visit His abode and our songs address His throne. How much is mercy His delight, O ever blessed God! How dear your servants are in your sight, how precious is their blood. How happy all your servants are! How great your grace is to us! My life, which you have made your care, Lord, I devote to you. Now we are yours, forever yours, nor shall our purpose move; your hand has loosed our bonds of pain and bound us with your love. Here in your courts, we leave our vow, and your rich grace record; Witness you saints who hear us now, if we forsake the Lord. Amen Ps. 116:12-19 (ESV)

Devotions for Thanks be to God.

Monday Luke 17:16 ESV

> *16 He threw himself at Jesus' feet and **thanked him**—and he was a Samaritan.*

Frequently the people closest to you are the very ones that forget to be grateful. Of all the people who were healed by Jesus, it was the one that was furthest from God, furthest from Jesus, furthest from the work of the Spirit, the Samaritan, who was healed and was grateful. You'd have thought the Jews who knew of God's work and were called the chosen people would have been the first and the deepest in their appreciation. What about us as God's church? Are we grateful for Jesus? For forgiveness? For eternal life? For the hope we have.

> **Activity**: Make a list of those gifts of God you have gotten recently. Tomorrow we will do something with them. Thank you, Father, for all the gifts you have showered down on me/us. Amen

Tuesday John 6:11,23 ESV

> *11 Jesus then took the loaves, **gave thanks**, and distributed to those who were seated as much as they wanted. He did the same with the fish. Then some boats from Tiberias landed near the place where the people had eaten the bread after **the Lord had given thanks**.*

Here we have the example set for us by Jesus. If Jesus, the Son of God gives thanks to the Father for His presence and provision in this moment for thousands of people crafted in His image, how much more should we who are in His image and have a relationship with Him. The firstborn of all creation sets the direction for us. We follow. His gratitude is for God's provision. Today, what has God provided for you and in fact with the qualifier, as much as you wanted. Do you have an abundance of grace? Do you have plenteous forgiveness of sin? Is your life overflowing with all God has given? How do you say thanks be to God in His goodness?

> **Activity:** Now take a bit of time and give thanks to God in prayer or by writing in a journal or by sharing with a friend, each of those precious gifts God has given. Thank you, Father, for ALL you have given and people to share it with. Amen

Wednesday Romans 1:8; Col. 1:4 (ESV)

> *⁸ First,* **I thank my God through Jesus Christ** *for all of you, because your faith is being reported all over the world.*
> *⁴ because we have heard of your faith in Christ Jesus and of the love you have for all God's people—*

Paul was grateful for people. These people were his fellow-travelers, people who were holding fast by faith to Jesus Christ. What is this faith for which Paul was so grateful? What is a faith that is reflective for the entire world? What kind of faith do we have, and would Paul be bragging about our faith to the rest of Christianity? This faith is deeply rooted, intensely personal and lived out vibrantly to all those around us. When the Church does this today, it gladdens the heart of those who are called by God, to walk with Him as a witness to His grace and love shown to us in Jesus Christ.

> **Thought:** Where do you have to grow in your faith so that it could achieve world renown and for which others would be grateful and thankful.

Thursday Colossians 2:7 (ESV)

*⁷ rooted and built up in him, strengthened in the faith as you were taught, and overflowing with **thankfulness.***

Being thankful for anything is rooted and growing in something. In other words, our faith should be growing up and out, should be bearing fruit and should be as strong as a California redwood. How deep is your faith rooted in the knowledge and life of Jesus Christ? What can you do to deepen those roots? You will know when your faith is deeper when the fruit it bears is overflowing with thankfulness to God for all His good gifts. Pause for a moment this week and thank God again for all that He draws to your mind and heart for which you can be thankful.

Thank you, Father, for all your good and perfect gifts that bring joy to my life. Amen

Friday Revelation 11:17 (ESV)

*¹⁷ saying: "**We give thanks** to you, Lord God Almighty, the One who is and who was, because you have taken your great power and have begun to reign.*

This text points us to where all our thanks and worship should go. The one who is and was and who has begun to reign, Jesus Christ. We owe EVERYTHING to Him. As you look forward to this next year, for what can you be thankful and what do you look forward to? In all of it thanks be to God for all He has done and given.

Activity: What can you look forward to that God has given to you already?

Saturday Luke 22:17 (ESV)

*¹⁷ After taking the cup, **he gave thanks** and said, "Take this and divide it among you.*

There is more than enough to go around. When we come to the table tomorrow it would be good for all of us to say thanks be to God for the plenteous grace, He has given to our congregation over the course of the past 80+ years and over the course of the past 10 years. God has given a plenteous grace through faith. Thanks be to God through our savior Jesus Christ.

> Activity: Now would be a suitable time to pray a prayer of confession for sin. It would also be a suitable time to get right with the people who share worship with you.

Sunday Romans 7:21-25 (ESV)

²¹ So I find this law at work: Although I want to do good, evil is right there with me. ²² For in my inner being I delight in God's law; ²³ but I see another law at work in me, waging war against the law of my mind and making me a prisoner of the law of sin at work within me. ²⁴ What a wretched man I am! Who will rescue me from this body that is subject to death? ²⁵ **Thanks be to God, who delivers me through Jesus Christ our Lord!**

As you come to the table today, bear in mind what you are to be truly and deeply thankful for. While in ourselves we are deeply and terribly broken by sin, and even continue that way as we strive to follow Jesus, thanks be to God we are rescued by the work of Jesus Christ on the cross. The body and blood we participate in today is a gift that rescues us from this body of sin and death. Thanks be to God through our savior and Lord Jesus Christ.

> Father, we come before you today grateful and thankful and praising your name in adoration for the work of your Son Jesus. Truly Eucharist.... Thanks be to you Father for all that you have done and given. Amen

God's Gift of Grace

Monday Genesis 3:21 (ESV) *The Lord God made garments of skin for Adam and his wife and clothed them.*

Grace means loving kindness in the Hebrew and gift in the Greek. Grace is part of God's character as well as action. It is who He is. In Genesis, in the face of humanities (Adam and Eve) sin, Yahweh (the Lord God) offers grace before judgment. That is the same way it works at Exodus and the same at the cross. God's gift of grace covers Adam, Eve, and humanity.

Prayer: Thank you Father for covering my sin by the blood of your Son Jesus in whose name I/we pray, Amen

Tuesday Exodus 34:6-7 (ESV) *And he passed in front of Moses, proclaiming, "The Lord, the Lord, the compassionate and gracious God, slow to anger, abounding in love and faithfulness, ⁷maintaining love to thousands, and forgiving wickedness, rebellion and sin. Yet he does not leave the guilty unpunished; he punishes the children and their children for the sin of the parents to the third and fourth generation."*

God not only passes over us but also passes in front of us. Who led Israel out of Egypt? God did! Who led Israel in battle to claim the promised land? God did! Who is ahead of us in all things, who is before us, the first born of all creation? God, in Christ is! The grace of God is in His leading, calling, saving, and protecting His children. Who is in front of you this week?

Activity: Before coming to the table this week, think of events, issues, or areas of your life where God needs to go first to show you the way.

Wednesday John 1:16-17 (ESV) *Out of his fullness we have all received grace in place of grace already given.* [17] *For the law was given through Moses; grace and truth came through Jesus Christ.*

Don't you dislike those gifts that you open, and, on the box, it says, "some assembly required"? It's almost as infuriating as getting a gift that is broken or has parts missing when you open it. John points out that God's grace is like none of those things listed above. God's grace is full, complete. The Greek word for full is full to overflowing. This fullness is of His love and forgiveness, grace, and compassion. The table is not a part, not a step in the right direction, not something to build on. It is the whole deal. God has done it all; no assembly required and nothing missing. When you come to the table this week come prepared for God to fill your life.

Prayer: Thank you Father for the fullness of grace measured out in the outstretched arms of your Son Jesus in whose name we pray, Amen.

Thursday - Ephesians 2:8-9 (ESV) *For it is by grace you have been saved, through faith—and this is not from yourselves, it is the gift of God—* [9] *not by works, so that no one can boast.*

How many gifts have you received, for all the different types of occasions that you take back because they do not fit, it is not your style, you just plain do not like it and so on? Grace is a gift of God. How many of us genuinely appreciate it, relish it, and in fact use it? If we are honest to God, it is a natural tendency to take grace for granted. Just like the Supper, we take it for granted. What does the Lord's Supper do? In the Lord's Supper we are fed by God, with the body of Christ. That is feeding on what gives us strength for the day and for life. Let us not take it for granted!

Activity: What in your diet gives you strength for each day? What in your spiritual diet gives you strength each day?

Friday - Titus 2:11-13 (ESV) [11] *For the grace of God has appeared that offers salvation to all people.* [12] *It teaches us to say "No" to ungodliness and worldly passions, and to live self-controlled, upright and godly lives in this present age,* [13] *while we wait for the blessed hope—the appearing of the glory of our great God and Savior, Jesus Christ.*

Saying YES to God's grace enables us to say NO to the world. In the supper we participate by Grace in the daily presence of the person of God in His Son Jesus. This prepares us for the time when we will be with Him for all eternity. The grace we say at the Supper is a grace of thanksgiving for God's gift of Himself to be always with us and in all places. When we come to the table in a couple of days, say grace for the gift of salvation that God has given in the body and blood of His Son Jesus.

<u>Prayer:</u> Thank you Father, for your Son Jesus in whom I/we have salvation. Remind me/us daily what we have been given and walk with us so that we may live godly lives. Amen

Saturday - Rom. 3:23-25 (ESV) *"for all have sinned and fall short of the glory of God, ²⁴ and all are justified freely by his grace through the redemption that came by Christ Jesus. ²⁵ God presented Christ as a sacrifice of atonement, through the shedding of his blood—to be received by faith. He did this to demonstrate his righteousness...*

Paul uses some weighty spiritual words here. Justified and atonement are big concepts. Here is the point. All of humanity, in every aspect of our humanity, is broken by sin. But all of humanity can be back in a relationship with God by His grace that sets us free. This is justification. This is possible because of the broken body and shed blood of the Son on the cross. That is atonement. As you approach the table, Give Thanks, (in the Greek Eucharist), praise God for His gift, and then live empowered, justified, and forgiven by His Son Jesus!

<u>Thought:</u> How can you live more freely (free from fear, free to serve, free for Christ), because of the work done by Jesus on the cross for you this week and the rest of your life?

Week of Good Friday

The Lamb of God

¹² And on the first day of Unleavened Bread, when they sacrificed the Passover lamb, his disciples said to him, "Where will you have us go and prepare for you to eat the Passover?"

The concept of preparation for communion was all new to me when I came into the Reformed family of Churches. Communion was thrown into a service because Jesus commanded it to be done to remember Him. Communion is just a memorial service. I learned differently as time passed. In this passage in Mark, we see Jesus seeking preparation for the Passover. This preparation was more than just getting a meal ready. It was a whole person's experience. The intent was to be ready to meet God in the one singular event that changed Hebrew history. By Good Friday will you be prepared to meet God? Start preparing today by getting right with God and others.

Prayer: Gracious and merciful God, draw me to you and then to others so that we all may find the life and vitality of Jesus Christ during this Easter season. Amen

Tuesday - John 1:29-36 (ESV)

²⁹ The next day he saw Jesus coming toward him, and said, "Behold, the Lamb of God, who takes away the sin of the world! ³⁰ This is he of

whom I said, 'After me comes a man who ranks before me, because he was before me.' [31] I myself did not know him, but for this purpose I came baptizing with water, that he might be revealed to Israel." [32] And John bore witness: "I saw the Spirit descend from heaven like a dove, and it remained on him. [33] I myself did not know him, but he who sent me to baptize with water said to me, 'He on whom you see the Spirit descend and remain, this is he who baptizes with the Holy Spirit.' [34] And I have seen and have borne witness that this is the Son[a] of God."

[35] The next day again John was standing with two of his disciples, [36] and he looked at Jesus as he walked by and said, "Behold, the Lamb of God!"

John the Baptist sees Jesus for who He really is. He is to be that Lamb of God for which we prepare. Like the lamb that Moses told the people to prepare for Passover, Jesus is that Lamb that will enable God to pass over our hearts and lives. He, Jesus, takes away the sins of the world. As we approach Good Friday, we as His people, should take a few moments to examine our faith like the Jews of that day. Do we really believe that we will receive life from God's hand? Do we really believe, that as believers, we shall be spared from the death we deserve and have life in the promised land that God gives? Good Friday is the gateway to that life for which we yearn.

Do: Make a list of your own sins that need to be hung on the tree this Friday. Begin today and work on through the week.

Wednesday - Acts 8:31-35 (ESV)

[31] And he said, "How can I, unless someone guides me?" And he invited Philip to come up and sit with him. [32] Now the passage of the Scripture that he was reading was this: "Like a sheep he was led to the slaughter and like a lamb before its shearer is silent, so he opens not his mouth. [33] In his humiliation justice was denied him. Who can describe his generation? For his life is taken away from the earth."

[34] And the eunuch said to Philip, "About whom, I ask you, does the prophet say this, about himself or about someone else?" [35] Then Philip opened his mouth, and beginning with this Scripture he told him the good news about Jesus.

We frequently come to the Word of God like the Eunuch in this passage. Could you please explain it to me; I do not get it. Interesting choice of passages for the Eunuch to read. Isaiah 53 is one of the key chapters of the Old Testament for us to understand the life of God handed over for us. Intended for the servant of God Israel in order that God's presence could be witnessed in the world of exile, the Eunuch sees a message for himself. Do you? Do we see this week as THE week of weeks in human history? Do we see the Lamb of God given by God for us to slaughtered for us and our sins? This passage is a key that opens the door to God's storehouse of grace and mercy. Take and open it this week and live.

Thought: How will you decisively leave your sins at the cross this year… and not pick them up again when you leave on Friday?

Thursday - 1 Corinthians 5: 6-8 (ESV)

[6] Your boasting is not good. Do you not know that a little leaven leavens the whole lump? [7] Cleanse out the old leaven that you may be a new lump, as you really are unleavened. For Christ, our Passover lamb, has been sacrificed. [8] Let us therefore celebrate the festival, not with the old leaven, the leaven of malice and evil, but with the unleavened bread of sincerity and truth.

I am not much of a baker. My Grandma and Mom did that as I was growing up. They made a lot of bread though. And I remember that the proportions of flour and eggs among other things was more than that tiny little packet of yeast. Yet that packet of yeast had a profound impact on the whole loaf. So, our sin has on us. It is not good enough to say we have gotten rid of it. Like the Jews of old we need to scour the whole of our lives the way they scoured all the house to rid it of every trace of yeast. Take a moment today to do a little scouring of your life. Are there corners of your mind, will, attitude and Spirit that you haven't looked in yet? Take another look!

Prayer: Father, open our eyes to every trace of sin that remains in us that tomorrow we may lay it all at your crucified feet. Forgive us for what we have done and for what we have forgotten we have done. Amen

Friday - 1 Peter 1:17-21(ESV)

[17] And if you call on him as Father who judges impartially according to each one's deeds, conduct yourselves with fear throughout the time of your exile, [18] knowing that you were ransomed from the futile ways inherited from your forefathers, not with perishable things such as silver or gold, [19] but with the precious blood of Christ, like that of a lamb without blemish or spot. [20] He was foreknown before the foundation of the world but was made manifest in the last times for the sake of you [21] who through him are believers in God, who raised him from the dead and gave him glory, so that your faith and hope are in God.

Today, when you approach the cross, it should seem strange to you. We are strangers here, Peter says. A symbol of execution is a strange way for a God of love to work His power over evil, sin and death. Kill death with death. Sacrifice something of infinite value for something of limited or no real value. Today, and not just for today but for all time, God, through the work of Jesus on the cross has turned everything upside down. Only God can do that. When you approach the cross tonight, approach it as if one who knows it does not make sense. It is not right for someone else to die for you. It's not right for you to have an abundant life at the expense of God whose life is filled with abundance. So, tonight, turn to the Lamb of God who takes away the sins of the world and live in Him.

Do: Tonight, come to the table and give up your sins on the cross. Be forgiven, but also forgive others who have sinned against you. Make this a night of reconciliation by the blood of the Lamb.

Lord's Supper Redemption

(This is the biblical foundation for an unformed liturgy. Using the texts that are provided, you can weave your liturgy according to the needs of the denomination, congregation, and worship service you are presenting on that particular day. Some of these texts will be used for your formulary, some for presentation and serving of the supper and some for the prayers that will be offered.)

Exodus 6:6 (**NASB95**)

[6] "Say, therefore, to the sons of Israel, 'I am the Lord, and I will bring you out from under the burdens of the Egyptians, and I will deliver you from their bondage. I will also redeem you with an outstretched arm and with great judgments.

Leviticus 25:24–28 (**NASB95**)

[24] 'Thus for every piece of your property, you are to provide for the redemption of the land. [25] 'If a fellow countryman of yours becomes so poor he has to sell part of his property, then his nearest kinsman is to come and buy back what his relative has sold. [26] 'Or in case a man has no kinsman, but so recovers his means as to find sufficient for its redemption, [27] then he shall calculate the years since its sale and refund the balance to the man to whom he sold it, and so return to his property. [28] 'But if he has not found sufficient means to get it back for himself, then what he has sold shall remain in the hands of its purchaser until the year of jubilee; but at the jubilee it shall revert, that he may return to his property.

Psalm 49:7–9 (**NASB95**)

[7] No man can by any means redeem his brother or give to God a ransom for him— [8] For the redemption of his soul is costly, and he should cease trying forever— [9] That he should live on eternally, that he should not undergo decay.

Psalm 130:7–8 (**NASB95**)

[7] O Israel, hope in the Lord; For with the Lord there is lovingkindness, And with Him is abundant redemption. [8] And He will redeem Israel from all his iniquities.

Isaiah 41:1–4 (**NASB95**)

[1] "Coastlands, listen to Me in silence, and let the peoples gain new strength; Let them come forward, then let them speak; Let us come together for judgment. [2] "Who has aroused one from the east Whom He calls in righteousness to His feet? He delivers up nations before him and subdues kings. He makes them like dust with his sword, As the wind-driven chaff with his bow. [3] "He pursues them, passing on in safety, by a way he had not been traversing with his feet. [4] "Who has performed and accomplished it, Calling forth the generations from the beginning? 'I, the Lord, am the first, and with the last. I am He.'"

Mark 10:45 (**NASB95**)

[45] "For even the Son of Man did not come to be served, but to serve, and to give His life a ransom for many."

Romans 3:24–25(NASB95)

[24] being justified as a gift by His grace through the redemption which is in Christ Jesus; [25] whom God displayed publicly as a propitiation in His

blood through faith. This was to demonstrate His righteousness, because in the forbearance of God He passed over the sins previously committed.

Galatians 4:4–7 (NASB95)

[4] But when the fullness of the time came, God sent forth His Son, born of a woman, born under the Law, [5] so that He might redeem those who were under the Law, that we might receive the adoption as sons. [6] Because you are sons, God has sent forth the Spirit of His Son into our hearts, crying, "Abba! Father!" [7] Therefore you are no longer a slave, but a son; and if a son, then an heir through God.

Ephesians 1:13–14 (NASB95)

[13] In Him, you also, after listening to the message of truth, the gospel of your salvation—having also believed, you were sealed in Him with the Holy Spirit of promise, [14] who is given as a pledge of our inheritance, with a view to the redemption of God's own possession, to the praise of His glory.

Colossians 1:13–14 (NASB95)

[13] For He rescued us from the domain of darkness and transferred us to the kingdom of His beloved Son, [14] in whom we have redemption, the forgiveness of sins.

Hebrews 9:11–15 (NASB95)

[11] But when Christ appeared as a high priest of the good things to come, He entered through the greater and more perfect tabernacle, not made with hands, that is to say, not of this creation; [12] and not through the blood of goats and calves, but through His own blood, He entered the holy place once for all, having obtained eternal redemption. [13] For if the blood of goats and bulls and the ashes of a heifer sprinkling those who have been defiled sanctify for the cleansing of the flesh, [14] how much more

will the blood of Christ, who through the eternal Spirit offered Himself without blemish to God, cleanse your conscience from dead works to serve the living God? [15] For this reason He is the mediator of a new covenant, so that, since a death has taken place for the redemption of the transgressions that were committed under the first covenant, those who have been called may receive the promise of the eternal inheritance.

1 Peter 1:18–19 (NASB95)

[18] knowing that you were not redeemed with perishable things like silver or gold from your futile way of life inherited from your forefathers, [19] but with precious blood, as of a lamb unblemished and spotless, the blood of Christ.

Devotions for The New Covenant

Sunday - Exodus 24:6-8 (ESV)

⁶ And Moses took half of the blood and put it in basins, and half of the blood he threw against the altar. ⁷ Then he took the Book of the Covenant and read it in the hearing of the people. And they said, "All that the LORD has spoken we will do, and we will be obedient." ⁸ And Moses took the blood and threw it on the people and said, "Behold the blood of the covenant that the LORD has made with you in accordance with all these words."

As you prepare for the new year, consider preparing through the new covenant made in blood. Moses reads the covenant to the people, the blood of the remembrance of Passover is sprinkled over the people and the people respond, "We will do everything the Lord has said; We will obey." What about us? As we prepare for a new year and new starts, do we also say we will do everything the Lord has said, we will obey. Of what does that obedience consist?

Monday Ezekiel 36:26-27; 37:24-28 (ESV)

²⁶ And I will give you a new heart, and a new spirit I will put within you. And I will remove the heart of stone from your flesh and give you a heart of flesh. ²⁷ And I will put my Spirit within you, and cause you to walk in my statutes and be careful to obey my rules.

²⁴ "My servant David shall be king over them, and they shall all have one shepherd. They shall walk in my rules and be careful to obey my statutes. ²⁵ They shall dwell in the land that I gave to my servant Jacob, where your fathers lived. They and their children and their children's children shall dwell there forever, and David my servant shall be their prince forever. ^{26} *I will make a covenant of peace with them. It shall be an everlasting covenant with them. And I will set them in their land and multiply them, and will set my sanctuary in their midst forevermore.* ^{27} *My dwelling place shall be with them, and I will be their God, and they shall be my people.* ^{28} *Then the nations will know that I am the* LORD *who sanctifies Israel, when my sanctuary is in their midst forevermore."*

Ezekiel writes about six hundred years after the account of Exodus. The people are not obedient. The people are not living out what God has commanded. Therefore, God will place a new heart within them. Our of the flock will come a lamb and He will be like David and of David. He will secure peace for God's people. Here we see Baptism renewed, restored, and reimaged in the life of God's people. We are being washed by the water of God and the Word of God and given a new heart we are made whole again. What areas of your life are dry and need the refreshing water of God?

Tuesday- Jeremiah 31:31-34 (ESV)

^{31} *"Behold, the days are coming, declares the* LORD, *when I will make a new covenant with the house of Israel and the house of Judah,* ^{32} *not like the covenant that I made with their fathers on the day when I took them by the hand to bring them out of the land of Egypt, my covenant that they broke, though I was their husband, declares the* LORD. ^{33} *For this is the covenant that I will make with the house of Israel after those days, declares the* LORD: *I will put my law within them, and I will write it on their hearts. And I will be their God, and they shall be my people.* ^{34} *And no longer shall each one teach his neighbor and each his brother, saying, 'Know the* LORD,' *for they shall all know me, from the least of them to the greatest, declares the* LORD. *For I will forgive their iniquity, and I will remember their sin no more."*

Jeremiah is a contemporary of Ezekiel. Jeremiah understands why God's people are judged by God and sent into exile. There has been an idolatry that offended God. There have been sins that pushed God's people away from Him and each other. For Jeremiah, the holiness and sovereignty of God are uppermost in his mind. What today constitutes idolatry? What do you idolize? Is it possible to come to the table and idolize anything other than God? Consider music, money, style, and the fact that this sentence may offend you.

Wednesday - 2 Corinthians 3:7-18 (ESV)

⁷ Now if the ministry of death, carved in letters on stone, came with such glory that the Israelites could not gaze at Moses' face because of its glory, which was being brought to an end, ⁸ will not the ministry of the Spirit have even more glory? ⁹ For if there was glory in the ministry of condemnation, the ministry of righteousness must far exceed it in glory. ¹⁰ Indeed, in this case, what once had glory has come to have no glory at all, because of the glory that surpasses it. ¹¹ For if what was being brought to an end came with glory, much more will what is permanent have glory. ¹² Since we have such a hope, we are very bold, ¹³ not like Moses, who would put a veil over his face so that the Israelites might not gaze at the outcome of what was being brought to an end. ¹⁴ But their minds were hardened. For to this day, when they read the old covenant, that same veil remains unlifted, because only through Christ is it taken away. ¹⁵ Yes, to this day whenever Moses is read a veil lies over their hearts. ¹⁶ But when one turns to the Lord, the veil is removed. ¹⁷ Now the Lord is the Spirit, and where the Spirit of the Lord is, there is freedom. ¹⁸ And we all, with unveiled face, beholding the glory of the Lord, are being transformed into the same image from one degree of glory to another. For this comes from the Lord who is the Spirit.

Paul connects the covenant in Jesus' blood with the covenant of stone and the blood of the lamb in this passage. This new covenant will not fade. This new covenant will not pass away. This new covenant is more glorious. This new covenant brings true freedom. This new covenant transforms lives. In what areas does your life need a makeover and how can this makeover, from sinner to God's child, be accomplished. How will you know if it is accomplished?

Thursday - Hebrews 8:6-12 (ESV)

⁶ But as it is, Christ has obtained a ministry that is as much more excellent than the old as the covenant he mediates is better, since it is enacted on better promises. ⁷ For if that first covenant had been faultless, there would have been no occasion to look for a second. ⁸ For he finds fault with them when he says: "Behold, the days are coming, declares the Lord, when I will establish a new covenant with the house of Israel and with the house of Judah, ⁹ not like the covenant that I made with their fathers on the day when I took them by the hand to bring them out of the land of Egypt. For they did not continue in my covenant, and so I showed no concern for them, declares the Lord. ¹⁰ For this is the covenant that I will make with the house of Israel after those days, declares the Lord: I will put my laws into their minds, and write them on their hearts, and I will be their God, and they shall be my people. ¹¹ And they shall not teach, each one his neighbor and each one his brother, saying, 'Know the Lord,' for they shall all know me, from the least of them to the greatest. ¹² For I will be merciful toward their iniquities, and I will remember their sins no more."

This letter reflects the absolute supremacy and sufficiency of Jesus Christ. In chapter 8 the writer talks of this high priest of the new covenant. There is a sense of superiority in this new covenant. The first covenant is now obsolete. The second covenant cut in the blood of Jesus which is like the first, is made sufficient and supreme. The sign of this new covenant is His blood. It is through His blood that we are made able to come to God. The goal of this is reconciliation with God through the work of Jesus. How are you able to stand before a Holy God?

Friday - Hebrews 9:11-15 (ESV)

¹¹ But when Christ appeared as a high priest of the good things that have come, then through the greater and more perfect tent (not made with hands, that is, not of this creation) ¹² he entered once for all into the holy places, not by means of the blood of goats and calves but by means of his own blood, thus securing an eternal redemption. ¹³ For if the blood of goats and bulls, and the sprinkling of defiled persons with the ashes of a heifer, sanctify for the purification of the flesh, ¹⁴ how much more will the blood of Christ, who through the eternal Spirit offered himself without blemish to God, purify our conscience from dead works to serve the living God. ¹⁵ Therefore he is the mediator of a new covenant, so that those who are called may receive the promised eternal inheritance, since a death has occurred that redeems them from the transgressions committed under the first covenant.

Now the writer of Hebrews moves from the priesthood to the sacrifice itself. The New Covenant is not just a matter of leadership but one of substance. Jesus, the Only Begotten Son of the living God, Holy, spotless and blameless, has been offered up for you a broken sinner who cannot help but continue to sin in the same fashion as the Israel of Jeremiah and Ezekiel. Jesus is the mediator of a new way, a ransom to set us free from the sins of the first covenant. How do you express this new freedom to God through Jesus?

Saturday - Hebrews 12:22-24; Matthew 26:28 (ESV)

²² But you have come to Mount Zion and to the city of the living God, the heavenly Jerusalem, and to innumerable angels in festal gathering, ²³ and to the assembly of the firstborn who are enrolled in heaven, and to God, the judge of all, and to the spirits of the righteous made perfect, ²⁴ and to Jesus, the mediator of a new covenant, and to the sprinkled blood that speaks a better word than the blood of Abel.

²⁸ for this is my blood of the covenant, which is poured out for many for the forgiveness of sins.

Now we are in a new place. The New Jerusalem, the new city of God to the Church of the firstborn. We have come through Jesus the mediator of a new covenant in His blood which was poured out for us. We have been sprinkled with this blood, that we might be to the praise of God's glory. Having once been cleansed by His blood what can destroy and taint. According to Paul in Romans 8:38-39 there is nothing that can separate us from this mediator once we have been claimed by Him. When you come to the table tomorrow, how will this assurance change how you look at God in Jesus Christ?

Devotions for Communion

The Lamb of God

Sunday-Genesis 22:1-8 (ESV)

After these things God tested Abraham and said to him, "Abraham!" And he said, "Here I am." ² *He said, "Take your son, your only son Isaac, whom you love, and go to the land of Moriah, and offer him there as a burnt offering on one of the mountains of which I shall tell you."* ³ *So Abraham rose early in the morning, saddled his donkey, and took two of his young men with him, and his son Isaac. And he cut the wood for the burnt offering and arose and went to the place of which God had told him.* ⁴ *On the third day Abraham lifted up his eyes and saw the place from afar.* ⁵ *Then Abraham said to his young men, "Stay here with the donkey; I and the boy will go over there and worship and come again to you."* ⁶ *And Abraham took the wood of the burnt offering and laid it on Isaac his son. And he took in his hand the fire and the knife. So they went both of them together.* ⁷ *And Isaac said to his father Abraham, "My father!" And he said, "Here I am, my son." He said, "Behold, the fire and the wood, but where is the lamb for a burnt offering?"* ⁸ *Abraham said, "God will provide for himself the lamb for a burnt offering, my son." So they went both of them together.*

If there is a more compelling and heart-rending story in the Bible, I am not sure what it would be. An aged man and a young boy head out to a mountain because God once again has beckoned. They are going to make a sacrifice. Everything necessary is handy, except the sacrifice. Where is the lamb? Put yourself in Abraham's place if you are or have been a parent and meditate on how you would respond. If you are a child, put yourself in Isaac's place. When does the realization dawn on you and how would you respond?

Monday-Exodus 12:1-11(ESV)

The LORD said to Moses and Aaron in the land of Egypt, [2] "This month shall be for you the beginning of months. It shall be the first month of the year for you. [3] Tell all the congregation of Israel that on the tenth day of this month every man shall take a lamb according to their fathers' houses, a lamb for a household. [4] And if the household is too small for a lamb, then he and his nearest neighbor shall take according to the number of persons; according to what each can eat you shall make your count for the lamb. [5] Your lamb shall be without blemish, a male a year old. You may take it from the sheep or from the goats, [6] and you shall keep it until the fourteenth day of this month, when the whole assembly of the congregation of Israel shall kill their lambs at twilight. [7] "Then they shall take some of the blood and put it on the two doorposts and the lintel of the houses in which they eat it. [8] They shall eat the flesh that night, roasted on the fire; with unleavened bread and bitter herbs they shall eat it. [9] Do not eat any of it raw or boiled in water, but roasted, its head with its legs and its inner parts. [10] And you shall let none of it remain until the morning; anything that remains until the morning you shall burn. [11] In this manner you shall eat it: with your belt fastened, your sandals on your feet, and your staff in your hand. And you shall eat it in haste. It is the LORD's Passover.

We have a challenging time relating to this event. We have not been in bondage or captivity like Israel, and we have not done what could be called hard servitude. The truth of the lamb and its blood can evade us. The exercise of faith, the obedience to God's call and will and the sacrifice that is made before the sacrifice is attempted are all examples to us of the lamb of God who goes to the cross for us.

Tuesday- Isaiah 53:1-7 (ESV)

Who has believed what he has heard from us? And to whom has the arm of the LORD been revealed? [2] For he grew up before him like a young plant, and like a root out of dry ground; he had no form or majesty that we should look at him, and no beauty that we should desire him.

³ He was despised and rejected by men, a man of sorrows and acquainted with grief and as one from whom men hide their face he was despised, and we esteemed him not. ⁴ Surely he has borne our griefs and carried our sorrows; yet we esteemed him stricken, smitten by God, and afflicted. ⁵ But he was pierced for our transgressions; he was crushed for our iniquities; upon him was the chastisement that brought us peace, and with his wounds we are healed. ⁶ All we like sheep have gone astray; we have turned—every one—to his own way; and the Lord has laid on him the iniquity of us all. ⁷ He was oppressed, and he was afflicted, yet he opened not his mouth; like a lamb that is led to the slaughter, and like a sheep that before its shearers is silent, so he opened not his mouth.

In this stirring poem that points to the sacrifice of God's people, Isaiah desires Israel to understand that they are to make this sacrifice on behalf of others daily. Each of them, like a lamb being led to slaughter is offered up for those who do not yet know God and His desire for them to be in relationship for them. When we put the face of Jesus on the suffering servant, we begin to see ourselves as the lamb who before his shearers is dumb, as a lamb led to slaughter, we give ourselves for others. Who do we need to give up our life to before this Lord's Supper celebration?

Wednesday- John 1:29-36 (ESV)

²⁹ The next day he saw Jesus coming toward him, and said, "Behold, the Lamb of God, who takes away the sin of the world! ³⁰ This is he of whom I said, 'After me comes a man who ranks before me, because he was before me.' ³¹ I myself did not know him, but for this purpose I came baptizing with water, that he might be revealed to Israel." ³² And John bore witness: "I saw the Spirit descend from heaven like a dove, and it remained on him. ³³ I myself did not know him, but he who sent me to baptize with water said to me, 'He on whom you see the Spirit descend and remain, this is he who baptizes with the Holy Spirit.' ³⁴ And I have seen and have borne witness that this is the Son of God."

John saw and knew Him for who He was. Behold the Lamb of God who takes away the sins of the world. The sacrifice God has prepared from the foundation of the world in His Son, is to be made once for all and not just a spotless lamb but the living Son of God. This sacrifice is not just for sins for this year but for all people for all time. And this sacrifice is God Himself giving of Himself for me. What have I done, who am I that Jesus died for me?

Thursday- 1 Peter 1:18-21(ESV)

¹⁸ knowing that you were ransomed from the futile ways inherited from your forefathers, not with perishable things such as silver or gold, ¹⁹ but with the precious blood of Christ, like that of a lamb without blemish or spot. ²⁰ He was foreknown before the foundation of the world but was made manifest in the last times for the sake of you ²¹ who through him are believers in God, who raised him from the dead and gave him glory, so that your faith and hope are in God.

The bottom line for Peter who sees Jesus as the Lamb of God is that our faith and our hope are grounded in Him. Jesus in the sacrifice points us to God, equips us to walk with God, reconciles us to God, intercedes before us with God, and provides us with God's Spirit so that we might have joy, strength peace and hope each day from God. When you come to the lamb this Lord's Supper, think about the God you believe in and what He has done for you.

Friday- Revelation 14:1-5 (ESV)

Then I looked, and behold, on Mount Zion stood the Lamb, and with him 144,000 who had his name and his Father's name written on their foreheads. ² And I heard a voice from heaven like the roar of many waters and like the sound of loud thunder. The voice I heard was like the sound of harpists playing on their harps, ³ and they were singing a new song before the throne and before the four living creatures and before the elders. No one could learn that song except the 144,000 who had been redeemed from the earth. ⁴ It is these who have not defiled themselves with women, for they are virgins. It is these who follow the Lamb wherever he goes. These have been redeemed from mankind as firstfruits for God and the Lamb, ⁵ and in their mouth no lie was found, for they are blameless

The Lamb and the 144,000. Who are these people? Wisdom tells us they are of the 12 tribes of the old Covenant and 12 disciples of the New Covenant who multiplied by a number too great to understand come out to be the perfect number of people whom God has set apart before the foundation of the world. The Lamb goes before them. These are the ones that followed the lamb wherever he went. As Jesus said follow me, so they did, being obedient to Him through His Spirit. These are the firstborns among many brothers. At the table, take fellowship with the lamb of God.

Saturday- Revelation 5:6-12 (ESV)

[6] And between the throne and the four living creatures and among the elders I saw a Lamb standing, as though it had been slain, with seven horns and with seven eyes, which are the seven spirits of God sent out into all the earth. [7] And he went and took the scroll from the right hand of him who was seated on the throne. [8] And when he had taken the scroll, the four living creatures and the twenty-four elders fell down before the Lamb, each holding a harp, and golden bowls full of incense, which are the prayers of the saints. [9] And they sang a new song, saying, "Worthy are you to take the scroll and to open its seals, for you were slain, and by your blood you ransomed people for God from every tribe and language and people and nation, [10] and you have made them a kingdom and priests to our God, and they shall reign on the earth." [11] Then I looked, and I heard around the throne and the living creatures and the elders the voice of many angels, numbering myriads of myriads and thousands of thousands, [12] saying with a loud voice, "Worthy is the Lamb who was slain, to receive power and wealth and wisdom and might and honor and glory and blessing!"

The lamb of Genesis that was provided to Abraham, the lamb that was taken from the poor man's house 2 Samuel 12, is the lamb of God who takes away the sins of the world. This lamb is worshiped as the only one who has the power to set creation and God's people free. In the Lord's Supper we celebrate that lamb as the one who is worthy to receive power and glory and honor and strength and wealth and wisdom and praise. Come to the table and praise God for His gift of His Son the Lamb who takes away our sins.

The cup of blessing and the cup of God's Wrath (A)

Good Friday Service devotions

Monday Isaiah 51:17-23(ESV)

[17] Wake yourself, wake yourself, stand up, O Jerusalem, you who have drunk from the hand of the LORD the cup of his wrath, who have drunk to the dregs the bowl, the cup of staggering.
[18] There is none to guide her among all the sons she has borne; there is none to take her by the hand among all the sons she has brought up. [19] These two things have happened to you— who will console you?— devastation and destruction, famine and sword; who will comfort you [20] Your sons have fainted; they lie at the head of every street like an antelope in a net; they are full of the wrath of the LORD, the rebuke of your God. [21] Therefore hear this, you who are afflicted, who are drunk, but not with wine: [22] Thus says your Lord, the LORD, your God who pleads the cause of his people: "Behold, I have taken from your hand the cup of staggering; the bowl of my wrath you shall drink no more; [23] and I will put it into the hand of your tormentors, who have said to you, 'Bow down, that we may pass over'; and you have made your back like the ground and like the street for them to pass over."

Have you ever been abused by someone, what is usually called you "have been walked all over"? You know, where people abuse and use you for their own selfish purposes? It does not feel good, does it? That is what Isaiah hears from God in this passage in Isaiah. The people of Israel have walked on God and those who torment and surround them will walk on

God's people. The reason is the cup of wrath. In a real sense, drinking this cup is like consuming alcohol. It makes the one who drinks reel, stagger, and fall. People can be what is called "drunk with power", ambition and success is to be wrapped up in one's own achievements. The people of God can be fully consumed by and caught up in God's achievement for them. That is the cross and the symbol of the cross is the cup and the bread. Don't walk on God and don't be walked on by the world; be filled by the cup of God's blessing.

Tuesday Jeremiah 49:12-16 (ESV)

¹² For thus says the LORD: "If those who did not deserve to drink the cup must drink it, will you go unpunished? You shall not go unpunished, but you must drink. ¹³ For I have sworn by myself, declares the LORD, that Bozrah shall become a horror, a taunt, a waste, and a curse, and all her cities shall be perpetual wastes." ¹⁴ I have heard a message from the LORD, and an envoy has been sent among the nations: "Gather yourselves together and come against her, and rise up for battle! ¹⁵ For behold, I will make you small among the nations, despised among mankind. ¹⁶ The horror you inspire has deceived you, and the pride of your heart, you who live in the clefts of the rock, who hold the height of the hill. Though you make your nest as high as the eagle's, I will bring you down from there, declares the LORD.

Here's another one of those passages that is difficult to understand. The issue is arrogance. When we take pride in our accomplishments, when we boast in our successes, it is then that God reminds what He has done and us who He is. Jesus is made to drink the cup which is a symbol of punishment for our resting in our own works and abilities. God comes to the people of Israel and encourages them to watch what happens to the other people around them when they rise and forget about God. Have you forgotten about God? Have you trusted in your own ability to walk with Him and have a relationship with Him? When you drink the cup this week, will it be a cup that reminds you of God's work for you or will it remind you of how good you have been so you can come to the table?

Wednesday Psalm 75:6-10 (ESV)

⁶ For not from the east or from the west and not from the wilderness comes lifting up, ⁷ but it is God who executes judgment, putting down one and lifting up another. ⁸ For in the hand of the LORD there is a cup with foaming wine, well mixed, and he pours out from it, and all the wicked of the earth shall drain it down to the dregs. ⁹ But I will declare it forever; I will sing praises to the God of Jacob. ¹⁰ All the horns of the wicked I will cut off, but the horns of the righteous shall be lifted up.

What a wonderful thing it is to need God. What a great gift to know to whom you belong, not because you have chosen Him, but because He has laid His hand and favor upon you! The opposite of this is to think that I have chosen Him and that I have made the right moves. There is a dramatic difference between arrogance and humility, between need and want. The Psalmist makes note of this fact. Some of the people of Israel have gotten to the point where they feel they deserve what they have gotten and want more. To those who are arrogant and lift their cups to be filled by God because they deserve it, the writer warns, "don't lift your horns to heaven, take care how you crane your neck as if to say you have no need, only want." We come to the table with an empty cup looking for God to fill it with His presence like a beggar who realizes that the only source of sustenance before him is God. Come to the table to be filled by God's Spirit because you need it desperately!

Thursday Zechariah 12:1-14 (ESV)

² "Behold, I am about to make Jerusalem a cup of staggering to all the surrounding peoples. The siege of Jerusalem will also be against Judah. ³ On that day I will make Jerusalem a heavy stone for all the peoples. All who lift it will surely hurt themselves. And all the nations of the earth will gather against it. ⁴ On that day, declares the LORD, I will strike every horse with panic, and its rider with madness. But for the sake of the house of Judah I will keep my eyes open, when I strike every horse of the peoples with blindness. ⁵ Then the clans of Judah shall say to themselves, 'The inhabitants of Jerusalem have strength through the LORD of hosts, their God.'

⁶ *"On that day I will make the clans of Judah like a blazing pot in the midst of wood, like a flaming torch among sheaves. And they shall devour to the right and to the left all the surrounding peoples, while Jerusalem shall again be inhabited in its place, in Jerusalem.*

⁷ *"And the* LORD *will give salvation to the tents of Judah first, that the glory of the house of David and the glory of the inhabitants of Jerusalem may not surpass that of Judah.* ⁸ *On that day the* LORD *will protect the inhabitants of Jerusalem, so that the feeblest among them on that day shall be like David, and the house of David shall be like God, like the angel of the* LORD, *going before them.* ⁹ *And on that day I will seek to destroy all the nations that come against Jerusalem.*

¹⁰ *"And I will pour out on the house of David and the inhabitants of Jerusalem a spirit of grace and pleas for mercy, so that, when they look on me, on him whom they have pierced, they shall mourn for him, as one mourns for an only child, and weep bitterly over him, as one weeps over a firstborn.*

The date is about five hundred years before Jesus. The people of Israel have been through numerous times of bondage and release. The law has proven ineffective in enabling them to have an on-going relationship with God. God will destroy all those that surround Jerusalem. One will be given and through Him God will pour out on the people the Spirit of grace. The suffering servant, Jesus, will be pierced for their sin. The theme of being poured out, usually with reference to bowls or cups of wine, has reference to being emptied on behalf of someone else. God wants so badly to have relationship with His creation that He is willing to be poured out so that we might be drawn back to Him. The land and all its inhabitants will mourn, and God will be vindicated; relationship will be restored. When you look at the cup this week, realize and mourn for there has been One who has been poured out for you.

Friday Matthew 26:36-39 (ESV)

³⁶ *Then Jesus went with them to a place called Gethsemane, and he said to his disciples, "Sit here, while I go over there and pray."* ³⁷ *And taking with him Peter and the two sons of Zebedee, he began to be sorrowful and troubled.* ³⁸ *Then he said to them, "My soul is very sorrowful, even to death; remain*

here, and watch[a] with me." ³⁹ And going a little farther he fell on his face and prayed, saying, "My Father, if it be possible, let this cup pass from me; nevertheless, not as I will, but as you will."

Well, it is time. Just like Good Friday coming up, here we see Jesus on this Friday's devotions crying out to God, that, if possible, let this cup pass from me. What cup? The cup of the wrath of God on the sins of humanity. My sin, all of it, the foulness and filth of a life lived apart from the grace of God made into a bitter liquid that Jesus will drink, rather than being poured down my own throat. My sin, the disgusting self-will of a life lived on my own, the distasteful bitter vetch of continuing errors of judgment and separation from God consumed in a swallow by Jesus. Then multiply that by hundreds and thousands and millions more. All that bitterness and filth, all that distasteful garbage, and even the best that I could do, an ugly mixed beverage for Jesus to drink. We would beg for this cup to pass from us, if we realized we would have to drink it. Yet, Jesus consumes it all on our behalf. How grateful we could and should be!

(For use when not used on Holy Week)

Saturday Revelation 14:8-19 (ESV)

⁸ Another angel, a second, followed, saying, "Fallen, fallen is Babylon the great, she who made all nations drink the wine of the passion of her sexual immorality." ⁹ And another angel, a third, followed them, saying with a loud voice, "If anyone worships the beast and its image and receives a mark on his forehead or on his hand, ¹⁰ he also will drink the wine of God's wrath, poured full strength into the cup of his anger, and he will be tormented with fire and sulfur in the presence of the holy angels and in the presence of the Lamb. ¹¹ And the smoke of their torment goes up forever and ever, and they have no rest, day or night, these worshipers of the beast and its image, and whoever receives the mark of its name." ¹² Here is a call for the endurance of the saints, those who keep the commandments of God and their faith in Jesus. ¹³ And I heard a voice from heaven saying, "Write this: Blessed are the dead who die in the Lord from now on." "Blessed indeed," says the Spirit, "that they may rest from their labors, for their deeds follow them!" ¹⁸ And another angel came out from the altar, the angel who has authority over the fire, and he called with a loud voice to the one who had the sharp sickle, "Put in your sickle and gather the clusters from the vine of the earth, for its grapes are ripe." ¹⁹ So the angel swung his sickle across the earth and gathered the grape harvest of the earth and threw it into the great winepress of the wrath of God.

What adulteries have we participated in that we need to drink to the dregs? Full strength, the people set apart from God will drink this bitter cup in the presence of the lamb and the angels, this mixture of a drink so bitter it destroys life. Blessed is the one, on the other hand, who die in the Lord. The cup of communion, our common fellowship with God through the blood of Christ, enables us to be blessed, for we have died to self through Him by grace and faith, and now live in fellowship with God through Jesus Christ. We don't have to drink the cup; it has been done for us by Jesus. Praise God for the gift of God that we are enabled to receive at His table.

Sunday Revelation 16:1-19 (ESV)

¹⁷ The seventh angel poured out his bowl into the air, and a loud voice came out of the temple, from the throne, saying, "It is done!" ¹⁸ And there were flashes of lightning, rumblings, peals of thunder, and a great earthquake such as there had never been since man was on the earth, so great was that earthquake. ¹⁹ The great city was split into three parts, and the cities of the nations fell, and God remembered Babylon the great, to make her drain the cup of the wine of the fury of his wrath.

Seven bowls have been poured out and the wrath of God against humanity and our sin is consumed. All those who have set themselves against God, all those who have committed adultery by consorting with any one of a number of other god's, all those who have made idols of any one of a number of other things, will find themselves having these bowls poured out upon them. Instead of Jesus drinking this cup for us, those who find themselves opposed to God, will have opportunity to indulge in their last drunken revelry which leads to a hangover of the worst kind, separation from God. When you come to the table this morning, put aside all those things that you would have a fling with, all those things you idolize, all those things that sit upon the throne of your life and drink the cup of blessing, the blood of our Lord Jesus Christ given for us, His sweetness for our bitterness.

Devotions for The Bread of Life

Sunday- Genesis 3:17-19(ESV)

¹⁷ And to Adam he said, "Because you have listened to the voice of your wife and have eaten of the tree of which I commanded you, 'You shall not eat of it,' cursed is the ground because of you; in pain you shall eat of it all the days of your life; ¹⁸ thorns and thistles it shall bring forth for you; and you shall eat the plants of the field. ¹⁹ By the sweat of your face you shall eat bread, till you return to the ground, for out of it you were taken; for you are dust, and to dust you shall return."

The first appearance of the Hebrew word for bread is here in the Genesis story. To this point, the life of the human being was found and fulfilled in God. Here the curse is pronounced upon humanity and man. Because of sin, by the sweat of our own labors we will find sustenance. Apart from God, our natural arena for choice, we attempt to work out our own salvation. It's no wonder we act so lost and confused. God is our sustenance; Jesus provides the bread by the act of the WORD in creation and is the bread of life by God's design. When you look at the bread next week, will you focus on your own work and designs, desires and efforts, or God's sustenance provided for you?

Monday- Genesis 14:18-20 (ESV)

¹⁸ And Melchizedek king of Salem brought out bread and wine. (He was priest of God Most High.) ¹⁹ And he blessed him and said, "Blessed be Abram by God Most High, Possessor of heaven and earth; ²⁰ and blessed be God Most High, who has delivered your enemies into your hand!"

The story of Melchezidek is without precedent or conclusion in scripture. We find this interesting and obviously powerful king mentioned only three times in the Bible. The other two references point back to this event in Genesis. What interests us at this moment is what the king of Salem brought with him as he came to Abraham. This priest of God, (the only Lord God Almighty), brought with him bread and wine. Again, we see bread as the source of life, in this case life of peace in the land that God had given him. The bread, as a gift, is God's given through this man as a sign of the fullness of life to be had in that place and for all time after. List the ways in which you understand Jesus to be the source of life for you.

Tuesday- Exodus 16: 3-7,14-26, (ESV)

3 and the people of Israel said to them, "Would that we had died by the hand of the Lord in the land of Egypt, when we sat by the meat pots and ate bread to the full, for you have brought us out into this wilderness to kill this whole assembly with hunger." 4 Then the Lord said to Moses, "Behold, I am about to rain bread from heaven for you, and the people shall go out and gather a day's portion every day, that I may test them, whether they will walk in my law or not. 5 On the sixth day, when they prepare what they bring in, it will be twice as much as they gather daily." 6 So Moses and Aaron said to all the people of Israel, "At evening you shall know that it was the Lord who brought you out of the land of Egypt, 7 and in the morning you shall see the glory of the Lord, because he has heard your grumbling against the Lord. For what are we, that you grumble against us?" 14 And when the dew had gone up, there was on the face of the wilderness a fine, flake-like thing, fine as frost on the ground. 15 When the people of Israel saw it, they said to one another, "What is it?" For they did not know what it was. And Moses said to them, "It is the bread that the Lord has given you to eat. 16 This is what the Lord has commanded: 'Gather of it, each one of you, as much as he can eat. You shall each take an omer according to the number of the persons that each of you has in his tent.'" 17 And the people of Israel did so. They gathered, some more, some less. 18 But when they measured it with an omer, whoever gathered much had nothing left over, and whoever gathered little had no lack. Each of them gathered as much as he could eat. 19 And Moses said to them, "Let no one leave any of it over till the morning." 20 But they did not listen to Moses.

Some left part of it till the morning, and it bred worms and stank. And Moses was angry with them. ²¹ Morning by morning they gathered it, each as much as he could eat; but when the sun grew hot, it melted. ²² On the sixth day they gathered twice as much bread, two omers each. And when all the leaders of the congregation came and told Moses, ²³ he said to them, "This is what the LORD *has commanded: 'Tomorrow is a day of solemn rest, a holy Sabbath to the* LORD*; bake what you will bake and boil what you will boil, and all that is left over lay aside to be kept till the morning.'" ²⁴ So they laid it aside till the morning, as Moses commanded them, and it did not stink, and there were no worms in it. ²⁵ Moses said, "Eat it today, for today is a Sabbath to the* LORD*; today you will not find it in the field. ²⁶ Six days you shall gather it, but on the seventh day, which is a Sabbath, there will be none."*

It is funny how God comes to His people even when they grumble. Before there was a golden calf (an idol to worship) there was hunger and a culture to worship. While they may have been slaves and even walking dead men, in their mind's eye as they travel as free people under God, they are worse off where they are than where they were. Amid their grumbling and complaining and idolization of a prior way of life that was not really life, God provides the staff of life, sustenance, manna, bread! Not only will this providence of God in manna sustain life, but they also have as much of it as is required for each day. There is no lack with God. He is the source and there is enough to go around. What are your needs today? In what ways are you inclined to go back to the way things used to be rather than live with all God provides?

Wednesday- Malachi 1:6-11

⁶ *"A son honors his father, and a servant his master. If then I am a father, where is my honor? And if I am a master, where is my fear? says the* LORD *of hosts to you, O priests, who despise my name. But you say, 'How have we despised your name?' ⁷ By offering polluted food upon my altar. But you say, 'How have we polluted you?' By saying that the* LORD*'s table may be despised. ⁸ When you offer blind animals in sacrifice, is that not evil? And when you offer those that are lame or sick, is that not evil? Present that to your governor; will he accept you or show you favor? says the* LORD *of hosts. ⁹ And now entreat the favor of God, that he may be gracious to us. With such a gift from your hand,*

will he show favor to any of you? says the Lord *of hosts.* *¹⁰ Oh that there were one among you who would shut the doors, that you might not kindle fire on my altar in vain! I have no pleasure in you, says the* Lord *of hosts, and I will not accept an offering from your hand.* *¹¹ For from the rising of the sun to its setting my name will be[a] great among the nations, and in every place incense will be offered to my name, and a pure offering. For my name will be great among the nations, says the* Lord *of hosts.*

I admit this is a hard text to understand. Why use this during a week of preparation if it's difficult? The central piece of furniture in the temple was the table where the sacrifice was laid. The priests are charged by God, with violating this table. They have defiled it by laying on it a sacrifice that is not worthy of God. They are trying to pass off on God in a religious fashion what they wouldn't ever try to pass off on their political leadership or the important people of their day. This passage uses the word defiled a lot. What does that mean? Fundamentally it means to alter. It then means that which was pure, has become polluted filthy and unclean. God has determined what he considers a proper sacrifice. It is not up to us to decide what is acceptable. –What does God require of us? What are we offering instead?

Thursday- Matthew 16:5-15 (ESV)

⁵ When the disciples reached the other side, they had forgotten to bring any bread. ⁶ Jesus said to them, "Watch and beware of the leaven of the Pharisees and Sadducees." ⁷ And they began discussing it among themselves, saying, "We brought no bread." ⁸ But Jesus, aware of this, said, "O you of little faith, why are you discussing among yourselves the fact that you have no bread? ⁹ Do you not yet perceive? Do you not remember the five loaves for the five thousand, and how many baskets you gathered? ¹⁰ Or the seven loaves for the four thousand, and how many baskets you gathered? ¹¹ How is it that you fail to understand that I did not speak about bread? Beware of the leaven of the Pharisees and Sadducees." ¹² Then they understood that he did not tell them to beware of the leaven of bread, but of the teaching of the Pharisees and Sadducees. ¹³ Now when Jesus came into the district of Caesarea Philippi, he asked his disciples, "Who do people say that the Son of Man is?" ¹⁴ And they said, "Some say John the Baptist, others say Elijah, and others Jeremiah or one of the prophets." ¹⁵ He said to them, "But who do you say that I am?"

What does the symbol of yeast mean from a scriptural point of view? This important symbol reflects the presence of impurity, not the pure bread of God, unleavened by any other influence. We discuss bread from a wonder bread point of view. Our exclusively physical frame of reference is not conducive to a good understanding of the spiritual things of God. The disciples have the same problem. What was the problem in the teaching of the pharisees or the Sadducees? The problem at its heart was a lack of faith trust and belief in Jesus as messiah and Son of God. Oh, it might involve legalism or false teachings, judgmentalism or many other individual concerns but it is, foundationally, a lack of faith. Where is the yeast in your life, your worship, your belief?

Friday John 6:5-14; 25-58 (ESV)

⁵ Lifting up his eyes, then, and seeing that a large crowd was coming toward him, Jesus said to Philip, "Where are we to buy bread, so that these people may eat?" ⁶ He said this to test him, for he himself knew what he would do. ⁷ Philip answered him, "Two hundred denarii worth of bread would not be enough for each of them to get a little." ⁸ One of his disciples, Andrew, Simon Peter's brother, said to him, ⁹ "There is a boy here who has five barley loaves and two fish, but what are they for so many?" ¹⁰ Jesus said, "Have the people sit down." Now there was much grass in the place. So the men sat down, about five thousand in number. ¹¹ Jesus then took the loaves, and when he had given thanks, he distributed them to those who were seated. So also the fish, as much as they wanted. ¹² And when they had eaten their fill, he told his disciples, "Gather up the leftover fragments, that nothing may be lost." ¹³ So they gathered them up and filled twelve baskets with fragments from the five barley loaves left by those who had eaten. ¹⁴ When the people saw the sign that he had done, they said, "This is indeed the Prophet who is to come into the world!"

THE BREAD OF LIFE DISCOURSE

There is so much here it's hard to know where to start. Let's connect some of the devotions for this week. There is the providence of God for

His people in vs. 5. There is Jesus as the source of life in vs. 27. There is the grumbling of the people in vs. 43. We find the people discussing defilement in vs. 52. Then we see God's people choose the yeast of the pharisees or whatever else was important to them rather than Jesus in vs. 66. Jesus is the bread of life. His body broken for us reflects more than just a sacrifice for our salvation; it is God's gift of His life in place of ours. We live because He lives. Every day we should be partaking of the bread of life, Jesus. By being in His Word and by living according to His word we reflect the living God to people around us. What new thing about God through Jesus did you learn from His word this week?

Saturday- 1 Corinthians 10:14-22 (ESV)

14 Therefore, my beloved, flee from idolatry. 15 I speak as to sensible people; judge for yourselves what I say. 16 The cup of blessing that we bless, is it not a participation in the blood of Christ? The bread that we break, is it not a participation in the body of Christ? 17 Because there is one bread, we who are many are one body, for we all partake of the one bread. 18 Consider the people of Israel:[a] are not those who eat the sacrifices participants in the altar? 19 What do I imply then? That food offered to idols is anything, or that an idol is anything? 20 No, I imply that what pagans sacrifice they offer to demons and not to God. I do not want you to be participants with demons. 21 You cannot drink the cup of the Lord and the cup of demons. You cannot partake of the table of the Lord and the table of demons. 22 Shall we provoke the Lord to jealousy? Are we stronger than he?

Tomorrow, we remember Jesus body and blood through the imagery of the feeding of the 5,000. When you come to the table tomorrow, what idols do you need to leave behind? In what fashion do we participate in the demonic, the worldly, the broken even as we come to God's table? The Church has struggled with unity and holiness ever since humanity has been removed from the garden and the immediate sense of God's presence and nearness to us . We imagine through our own work we will achieve our sustenance. We forget that God has made provision for us through Jesus His Son. When you come to the table tomorrow, remember Him, His work, His word, and His life given in your place so that you may be lifted up with Him by God's grace.

Week of Preparation for Communion

The Messengers of God

December 5-11

"Comfort, comfort my people, says your God. [2] *Speak tenderly to Jerusalem, and cry to her that her warfare*[a] *is ended, that her iniquity is pardoned, that she has received from the LORD's hand double for all her sins.* [3] *A voice cries: "In the wilderness prepare the way of the LORD; make straight in the desert a highway for our God.* [4] *Every valley shall be lifted up, and every mountain and hill be made low; the uneven ground shall become level, and the rough places a plain.* [5] *And the glory of the LORD shall be revealed, and all flesh shall see it together, for the mouth of the LORD has spoken."* Isa. 40:1-5

This week as we prepare to come to the Lord's table, we are called back to the scripture of preparation for God's covenant people. As Paul encourages the Church at Corinth to prepare themselves to come to the table, so God has called His people to prepare their hearts. The messengers of God through all scripture have called God to prepare their hearts to receive the gift of God by grace. As you go through this week, prepare your hearts by coming home to God through His Word of life and grace Jesus.

Monday December 5 Genesis 19:15-17 [15] *As morning dawned, the angels urged Lot, saying, "Up! Take your wife and your two daughters who are here, lest you be swept away in the punishment of the city."* [16] *But he lingered. So the men seized him and his wife and his two daughters by the hand, the LORD being merciful to him, and they brought him out and set him outside the city.* [17] *And as they brought them out, one said, "Escape for your life. Do not look back or stop anywhere in the valley. Escape to the hills, lest you be swept away."*

Tuesday December 6 Genesis 24: 7 *⁷ The* LORD, *the God of heaven, who took me from my father's house and from the land of my kindred, and who spoke to me and swore to me, 'To your offspring I will give this land,' he will send his angel before you, and you shall take a wife for my son from there.*

Wednesday December 7 Luke 1:10-17 *¹⁰ And the whole multitude of the people were praying outside at the hour of incense. ¹¹ And there appeared to him an angel of the Lord standing on the right side of the altar of incense. ¹² And Zechariah was troubled when he saw him, and fear fell upon him. ¹³ But the angel said to him, "Do not be afraid, Zechariah, for your prayer has been heard, and your wife Elizabeth will bear you a son, and you shall call his name John. ¹⁴ And you will have joy and gladness, and many will rejoice at his birth, ¹⁵ for he will be great before the Lord. And he must not drink wine or strong drink, and he will be filled with the Holy Spirit, even from his mother's womb. ¹⁶ And he will turn many of the children of Israel to the Lord their God, ¹⁷ and he will go before him in the spirit and power of Elijah, to turn the hearts of the fathers to the children, and the disobedient to the wisdom of the just, to make ready for the Lord a people prepared."*

Thursday December 8 Luke 1:26-32 *²⁶ In the sixth month the angel Gabriel was sent from God to a city of Galilee named Nazareth, ²⁷ to a virgin betrothed to a man whose name was Joseph, of the house of David. And the virgin's name was Mary. ²⁸ And he came to her and said, "Greetings, O favored one, the Lord is with you!"[b] ²⁹ But she was greatly troubled at the saying, and tried to discern what sort of greeting this might be. ³⁰ And the angel said to her, "Do not be afraid, Mary, for you have found favor with God. ³¹ And behold, you will conceive in your womb and bear a son, and you shall call his name Jesus. ³² He will be great and will be called the Son of the Most High. And the Lord God will give to him the throne of his father David,*

Friday December 9 Luke 2:9-14 *⁹ And an angel of the Lord appeared to them, and the glory of the Lord shone around them, and they were filled with great fear. ¹⁰ And the angel said to them, "Fear not, for behold, I bring you good news of great joy that will be for all the people. ¹¹ For unto you is born this day in the city of David a Savior, who is Christ the Lord. ¹² And this will be a sign for you: you will find a baby wrapped in swaddling cloths and lying* *in a manger." ¹³ And suddenly there was with the angel a multitude of the heavenly host praising God and saying, ¹⁴ "Glory to God in the highest, and on earth peace among those with whom he is pleased!"*

Saturday December 10 Revelation 11:15-19 *¹⁵ Then the seventh angel blew his trumpet, and there were loud voices in heaven, saying, "The kingdom of the world has become the kingdom of our Lord and of his Christ, and he shall reign forever and ever." ¹⁶ And the twenty-four elders who sit on their thrones before God fell on their faces and worshiped God, ¹⁷ saying, "We give thanks to you, Lord God Almighty, who is and who was, for you have taken your great power and begun to reign. ¹⁸ The nations raged, but your wrath came, and the time for the dead to be judged, and for rewarding your servants, the prophets and saints, and those who fear your name, both small and great, and for destroying the destroyers of the earth." ¹⁹ Then God's temple in heaven was opened,*

X

The Difference a more regular celebration of the Lord's Supper can make!

Having gone through all of this material which points to a new way of celebrating the Lord's Supper, what can you expect to happen in your congregation and the lives of the individuals that accept the challenge of meeting Jesus regularly at Worship and at the table? After all, why go through the trouble, the time, the writing of worship services, devotions and liturgy and the worship effort if you would expect nothing positive or helpful to the discipleship of God's people to result? Is there more that is likely to happen that will enhance the spiritual life of God's people we serve, and the ministry of the body where we worship?

I suspect the next question(s) may be the most important question to answer from a human point of view. After all, we'd like to know what is in it for us (the church) and what we can expect to get out of it. Why would we change anything in our church, if it's not going to enhance ministry and make things better?

All these expectations are based, not on the program of devotions or on the material that is written but solely and merely on the power of the Word and Spirit of God. It is NEVER about what we do but only about what God wants for us and what He alone can do. Let's be clear, what has been proposed is not either a sure-fire program or method nor a guaranteed style that will produce desired results. It is intended to be an obedience to the call and will of God and therefore entrusts Him and Him alone for the results. Having said that you should know what to look for when you invest your time and congregation in this process.

Going back to the text in Luke 24 that we have already looked at, we see several results in the encounter with God through the Supper. First, eyes are opened to the presence, power and glory of God. Whenever the Word of God is present, it brings the fruit that is promised. God wants people to know Him personally and come back to Him in relationship. It should come as no surprise that the disciples who were on the road to Emmaus' eyes were open, and they finally understood who had been with them the whole time. The recognition is not merely physical but one of familiarity with the person who did the work of God for the people of God. I think we have a right to expect the same results in people's lives when the Lord's Supper is served.

Then their sadness (vs. 17) turned to joy (vs. 34-35). Can you imagine the ecstasy in your people individually or hopefully the congregation as a whole (ecstasy means in the original Greek, to be outside oneself) at knowing that what has happened is real, eternal and able to save! This alone would be a boon to many congregations in our day. The sheer joy of knowing. The sheer joy of participating in it. The sheer joy of not having to produce this for us but that it is the gift of God given to us. Rejoice the Lord is King!!

Beyond that there is the hope in the Biblical sense of an expectation, and power of enthusiasm which should also ensue. The word enthusiasm comes straight out of the Greek, En= in, thus=God and ism, an in-God ism or perhaps put more plainly, a passionate excitement about who God is and more than that who God is in ME! In the Luke 24 passage that enthusiasm led the disciples to go back to Jerusalem, at night, running up hill to bring the message that there was meaning and power behind the events of what we call passion week. They are filled with a story that is outside themselves, that empowers them to a holy boldness and expresses itself in a life that wants to bring life to others.

Then, there is the clarity about who God is and what He has done for us all encapsulated in the meal. These disciples recite facts about God, His will, His work and the consequence of all of that in their own lives. Jesus gives these facts meaning. Finally, they understand. What has happened and what God has initiated by the breaking of the bread has now become clear *FOR* and *IN* them. They are no longer lost and alone; without purpose in the world but they now have a sense of meaning in their lives. Through the supper and through the lens of the many distinct aspects of God's character and work we can begin to give that same clarity to our people.

The disciples before the breaking of the bread had vain hopes, (vs.21). There is nothing quite sadder than vain hope or hopelessness. The disciples find when the bread is broken that their hope is fulfilled in the lamb of calvary. As they had hoped in the religion of Abraham and Isaac, (see John 8) they now found the fulfillment in the Son of God crucified, the lamb that God provided for them, Jesus Christ. Can you foresee a day when the hopes of all your people, the hopes and dreams of all the years find fulfillment in Jesus Christ? Bringing this hope comes in the form of the Lord's Supper that is broken for us.

Their hearts burned within them. There is a power in the Word of God. Placed alongside the sacrament there is a renewed power. That power is the presence of God in the Holy Spirit. We ought to believe it by the power of experience, not just learning it. The disciples in this passage experienced the power of the presence of the living God. This power fundamentally changed them. They had their character shaped by it but also their behavior, as we will see in the next paragraph. What would it be like for your congregation to have their hearts burn within them because of the presence of the living God in the Holy Spirit? We are in the business of changed lives! This fire of devotion as scripture points out can lead to a new purity, can test and prove us for the work that God is giving to us.

Finally, this confrontation with the living God that has given them hope, life, renewal, and joy, also sees them doing something with it; they go and tell. The immediacy reflects the power of the living God moving in their lives. They shrug off all perils of the upcoming journey back to Jerusalem, (robbers, violence, death). They share their experience of the living God. They proclaim the living Christ. Now, think about what that would mean to your congregation and your worship. Robert Webber was fond of saying that the act of worship was an act of evangelism. Having been in the presence of the creator God, our response can and should be to tell the world. Tell them what? Our joy, our hope, our salvation, and forgiveness. Leaving worship would no longer be a sense of self-satisfaction but one of impelling us to share what we had been given by God.

These seven consequences together should encourage us to think about carefully and then plan carefully to come to the Lord's table more regularly and with more intentionality in our discipleship. Would we have more life in the Church? Would we have more power in the Church? Would we have a hope that the world cannot give? Then let us blend God's Word and God's act for us together and share that with the world.

XI

Frequently Asked Questions

❖ **What do I do with resistance from leadership, elders, or council?**

This is more of an administrative question than something within the purview of this book. However, the rule is that the Elders oversee spiritual matters which includes worship and therefore the Lord's Supper. That being the case, it is essential to get them on board. I would share with them the last chapter of the book. People like to know how change will benefit them. Second, I would go back to the devotions shared in the sixth chapter of the book. After a period of time in the Word of God, approach them again. Resistance to God is best met with God's Word. It is what Jesus did. Be patient. Use the time to prepare yourself for the moment when they say yes. Have liturgy and a devotional for the week, ready to share with them.

❖ **Does the variety of themes work against the commitment to memory and heart of the traditional liturgy?**

There is good news and difficult news with this question. Allow me a story to begin. My mother-in-law was afflicted with dementia/Alzheimer's later in life. She was a devout Christian and had not only much of scripture memorized but also a considerable number of hymns, at least the first verses of them. As a part of this lifelong process of sitting in worship of her God, she had also committed to memory parts of the worship experience including the liturgy of the supper. For someone like this, it was a real blessing to have not only the Word of God but the way to approach God and be blessed by God in the liturgy she had grown up with, committed to heart. I have no doubt that, while thematic communion would have been a blessing to her, it might also have been frustrating. Care should be taken then with doing communion "regularly" in the thematic style. In my opinion, going back to the standard form of whatever denomination to which you belong should be used. Our task again is not to amaze people with our creativity or ability but to lead ALL of them into God's presence to be fed by Him. Sensitivity by the pastor and leadership need to be exercised when moving into this new area.

❖ **Is there a certain style of worship that works best with this model of communion celebration?**

Frankly, I believe this style of communion celebration should work with ALL forms of worship. It would seem from the historical record which First Corinthians confirms that there was a time of preparation, (which may not have been as long as the week we have proposed), the meal and the Word whenever people gathered. This appears to be consistent throughout the churches, and regardless of setting. It should be admitted that the style of worship in the early church was simpler than ours. Liturgy, like the stuff in grandma's attic accumulates over time. All that being said, whether you are low church (informal and open liturgy) or high church, (a very formalized liturgy), the integration of thematic devotions paired with the thematic liturgy should be effective.

❖ **If we do this every week, doesn't that mean an entire year of devotionals prepared?**

It does! There is good news in this if you think about it. We have an opportunity to impact our congregations in the form of an on-going discipleship week to week, series to series, season to season, in a way that brings the entire Word of God to the people of God. Of course, the downside is the production of devotions for each day of the year. Since the Word of God is the bread of life from God, and since we are the shepherds that are to feed the flock, would it not be constructive for our people to fed daily on God's Word to be strengthened for the task that is set before them? And who better to do that than the shepherd closest to the flock? Well-fed sheep are not fat sheep, they are productive sheep. This should be good for evangelism, strength in the face of a culture that seems determined to take us down a briar path and over a cliff into constant idolatry and spiritual death. I don't see this as a problem but as an opportunity.

❖ What does this do to my preaching schedule?

There need not be any interruption in a preaching schedule. Regardless of if you do communion quarterly or monthly, or bi-monthly, or weekly, the addition of a thematic expression of the supper can be used. The assumption I am making is that you are preaching biblically. Since the themes of communion are all drawn from scripture, the whole counsel of God, the thematic expression of the Lord's supper can only enhance the preaching as well as the worship.

❖ Do I have to do the devotions and liturgy the way described in the book?

The material of this book, especially chapter six, are provided only as guidance not the only way. I wrote about devotions and liturgy provided in chapter 8, I wrote the way that was comfortable to me. What is most important to glean from chapter 6 and the entirety of this book is the necessity of this work in worship and then a framework for how to do this on a regular basis. The design was given for you to conform to scripture first. Secondarily, the liturgy was written to satisfy MOST denominations perhaps with some addition or subtraction on your part. Third, it is written to give each person who uses this the flexibility to make it work in their own context.

❖ Are there other themes that could be developed from Scripture?

I am sure there are. I have not done this exhaustively, but expediently. Some of the themes were easy and written about in my doctoral work. Others themes were added over the years as more thought was given and opportunities presented themselves. Others were added with an eye toward fitting it in to a certain theme of a service. I'm sure, as this concept ages, there will be people far more Biblical, theological and creative than I am who will find other themes that work just as good. The more you cultivate a passion for God's Word to know Him better and cultivate a sense of the Word of God in a unitary sense (not old Covenant and new Covenant separated by any number of historical events or ideas), you will begin to derive an eye toward what God has been leading us in and trying to help us see since the garden and which is still true all the way until He comes again.

❖ **Does coming to the table each week smack of being "Roman Catholic"?**

While it is true that for a Roman Catholic the Mass is central to their approach to God and worship of Him it is also something that we need to look at without a jaundiced eye toward all things "Catholic" being wrong for a protestant. For John Calvin, the Lord's Table could be approached every time the Word of God was preached, and he would preach every day. That sounds an awful lot like what we ought to expect for all eternity. Imagine being in God's presence and declining the opportunity to talk to Him, thank Him, get to know Him better and then also refuse the invitation to dine with Him on the food which He has laid before us! It feels like for much of the Church today, we want to be saved but we don't want to know the savior. We would like to live forever but on our own terms in our own manner. Since God is the author of life and since Jesus is the way to that life, it would seem to me that we would want more of that not less. Since the table and worship, is part of the fulfillment of what Jesus offers us to pray, "on earth as it is in heaven", it means to me that every opportunity I have to get to know Him more and to be in fellowship with Him is just one more moment of gratitude, joy and fullness. I believe that is what we can promote and experience with a regular experience of and celebration of the Lord's Supper.

❖ ***Does celebrating communion weekly make it "no longer special"?***

That is the conventional wisdom. What we need to do is reveal to people the eternal reality that is promoted by and reflected in the Lord's Supper as well as Passover. Think of it this way. Scripture says that we are a household of God. He is the Father. We have a Brother, Jesus. Households dine. They talk. They work together for a common good. Therefore, communion here on

Paul A. Hansen

earth is a foretaste of what it will be like forever with the Father and the Son in heaven. We have an eternity to dine with and on God. To have a frequent example and experience of that opportunity to dine with God through the work of His Son here on earth and experience the wonder of God and to give thanks for this meal that is given solely by grace for our benefit is not something we should ever see as mundane. In fact, I believe if done constantly revealing the person and work of the triune God, it can become more special each time we come to the table.

❖ **Can I do thematic communion part of the year, then "non-thematic" (denominationally designated liturgical) communion during other busier seasons?**

The answer is a resounding yes. In fact, I would encourage the practitioner to use the denominational forms they have access to on a regular basis to remind people of the greater Church to which they belong. In fact, with reference to the prior question, I believe that would make the Lord's Supper more special and would broaden our understanding of the Church. However, I would also suggest this. Using themes for communion can become a discipling opportunity for other lay members of the congregation. It may allow us to help those creative, natural theologians in our churches to use their gifts in a new way and for them to draw closer to God because of the writing. This could be a growth point for some in the church.

❖ **Does it matter how we distribute the elements (order, single loaf, leavened/unleavened bread, individual cups, common cup, juice, wine)?**

This is a tricky question. I remember when a young people's group on a retreat celebrated communion without the oversight of elders. They used pizza and Coke for the elements. Some find that disrespectful and less than authentic to the text of scripture whether Old or New Covenant. Care for God's gifts to us, as the body of Christ, should be exercised by those leading in the celebration, when coming to the table of God. We are not at liberty to deviate from the Biblical model and form which we have been given by God. However, in the examples given in the question, there is latitude. Whether one uses leavened or unleavened bread, breads of assorted colors, (rye, wheat and white for example) gluten free bread, wafers, and then grape juice or wine and then what kind of wine are choices that should be made by a board of elders with the pastor, and then informing the congregation of what is happening and why. In Reformed polity, it is the eldership that directs worship and the spiritual life of the congregation. Care should be taken to not step over that line to be Avant Garde.'

❖ **Can we do intinction with thematic communion liturgy?**

As with the prior question, I would leave this under the heading of follow the leading of the elders and inform the congregation. Intinction is one way of serving when people are encouraged to come forward. It can be very meaningful to some and can be effective with time usage in worship services that can become quite lengthy.

❖ **Should I mention the theological difference between Lutheran, Roman Catholic, Evangelical (Baptist, community Churches, Pentecostal), and Reformed during communion?**

I personally would avoid this practice during the celebrating of the supper. It can be pejorative, could damage evangelistic efforts by demeaning or denigrating other backgrounds and practices in which they were raised and have faith. If there is to be an explanation of theological differences, better to do that by using the biblical devotions during the week and better than that in my opinion would be to talk about the Lord's Supper in a class that would explain the biblical and theological meaning behind what we understand to be an essential of Christian Worship.

❖ **Does the scripture support coming to the table each week? What about the ancient "pre-Roman Catholic" Church?**

There are a several texts that I feel support the coming to the table to celebrate each week. At the end of the answer, I will also provide a couple historical quotes from first century theologians. Below you will find Matthew 26:26-29 first, then Acts 2:42 and then 1 Corinthians 11:17-34, a longer section of what Paul finds transpiring in one of the Churches he began and what they were doing with it. There will be a brief comment after both texts are translated. While none of these texts would indicate a divine command or mandate to come to the table each week, there is a connectedness between the Word, the fellowship and communion of the body of Christ, and the dining together as that body and the participation in the body of Christ. This answer is extremely long due to the commentary on each text as well as the shallow dive into the first Churches understanding of the Lord's table and how it fit into weekly worship.

Matthew 26:26-29

26 **Ἐσθιόντων δὲ αὐτῶν λαβὼν** ὁ Ἰησοῦς ἄρτον καὶ εὐλογήσας ἔκλασεν καὶ δοὺς τοῖς μαθηταῖς εἶπεν· Λάβετε φάγετε, τοῦτό ἐστιν τὸ σῶμά μου. 27 καὶ λαβὼν ποτήριον καὶ εὐχαριστήσας ἔδωκεν αὐτοῖς λέγων· Πίετε ἐξ αὐτοῦ πάντες, 28 τοῦτο γάρ ἐστιν τὸ αἷμά μου τῆς διαθήκης τὸ περὶ πολλῶν ἐκχυννόμενον εἰς ἄφεσιν ἁμαρτιῶν· 29 λέγω δὲ ὑμῖν, οὐ μὴ πίω ἀπ᾽ ἄρτι ἐκ τούτου τοῦ γενήματος τῆς ἀμπέλου ἕως τῆς ἡμέρας ἐκείνης ὅταν αὐτὸ πίνω μεθ᾽ ὑμῶν καινὸν ἐν τῇ βασιλείᾳ τοῦ πατρός μου. *(SBL Greek New Testament)*

26 While they were eating, Jesus took some bread, and [a]after a blessing, He broke it and gave it to the disciples, and said, "Take, eat; this is My body." 27 And when He had taken a cup and given thanks, He gave it to them, saying, "Drink from it, all of you; 28 for this is My blood of the covenant, which is poured out for many for forgiveness of sins. 29 But I say to you, I will not drink of this fruit of the vine from now on until that day when I drink it new with you in My Father's kingdom." (ESV)

There are a couple of things in this passage that indicate that the Lord's Supper is something we should seriously consider serving each week. First, is the use of the words de esthioton, while they were in the process of already eating. During the meal, Jesus takes the bread. A parallel might be while they were dining on the Word of God (reading of scripture and the sermon) they sat down to be addressed and blessed by Jesus. That leads us to the second word, bless, in the Greek Eulogeo and in the Hebrew Barakah. The word in the Hebrew, which should be more consequential since it would have been the word Jesus used, means to bow down before to worship and adore. We understand what bowing before God or blessing Him for His work and person is all about. The bowing of Jesus in the incarnation, which is God leaving heaven and dwelling with us, Philippians 2:5-11 and John 1:14, is going to be found in its final victory in His bowing His head on the cross. It is to both, this blessing points. The offering of blessing while we are dining, is a profound gift of God not to be missed amid dining on the Word of God.

The next passage in First Corinthians helps make clear what Paul sought to leave as his understanding of what God was to be to us because of what He has done for us.

Acts 2:42

42 ἦσαν δὲ προσκαρτεροῦντες τῇ διδαχῇ τῶν ἀποστόλων καὶ τῇ κοινωνίᾳ, τῇ κλάσει τοῦ ἄρτου καὶ ταῖς προσευχαῖς. *(SBL Greek New Testament)*

42 They were continually devoting themselves to the apostles' teaching and to fellowship, to the breaking of bread and to prayer. (ESV)

Here is one of the earliest biblical examples of how the people of the New Israel of God came together. We cannot understand the worship of the early Church without first considering what the Jewish community that was following Jesus would consider appropriate for glorifying, praising and thanking God for who He is and what He had done for them. There are four elements listed that will indicate what the people did in worship. They devoted themselves to God and His Word. The word devote means to attach to wait on, be faithful to someone. In this case, the WORD Jesus Christ. That would have included for them the scriptures of the Old Covenant. One could say that the people were busily engaged in and with God's WORD. This is seen in their lives daily and it could be argued moment by moment as a personal activity in addition to daily as a corporate activity is not born out by scripture. This passage through Church history has been seen either way. This devotion was to the WORD, and the fellowship, which is the gathering together of God's people in this case in Jerusalem and in or near the temple complex, and then to the breaking of bread which is our focus here. In another section we will discuss prayers as a part of this worship.

Paul A. Hansen

The phrase, "the breaking of bread" is significant. It is similar word usage and phraseology that is found in Luke 24 with the disciples on the road to Emmaus. Breaking of the bread is part of the worship/devotional gathering of the body of Christ. Along with the prayers and the immersion in the WORD, the meal fellowship was integral and a companion to the other activities.

1 Corinthians 11:17-34

17 Τοῦτο δὲ παραγγέλλων οὐκ ἐπαινῶ ὅτι οὐκ εἰς τὸ κρεῖσσον ἀλλὰ εἰς τὸ ἧσσον συνέρχεσθε. 18 πρῶτον μὲν γὰρ συνερχομένων ὑμῶν ἐν ἐκκλησίᾳ ἀκούω σχίσματα ἐν ὑμῖν ὑπάρχειν, καὶ μέρος τι πιστεύω. 19 δεῖ γὰρ καὶ αἱρέσεις ἐν ὑμῖν εἶναι, ἵνα καὶ οἱ δόκιμοι φανεροὶ γένωνται ἐν ὑμῖν. 20 συνερχομένων οὖν ὑμῶν ἐπὶ τὸ αὐτὸ οὐκ ἔστιν κυριακὸν δεῖπνον φαγεῖν, 21 ἕκαστος γὰρ τὸ ἴδιον δεῖπνον προλαμβάνει ἐν τῷ φαγεῖν, καὶ ὃς μὲν πεινᾷ, ὃς δὲ μεθύει. 22 μὴ γὰρ οἰκίας οὐκ ἔχετε εἰς τὸ ἐσθίειν καὶ πίνειν; ἢ τῆς ἐκκλησίας τοῦ θεοῦ καταφρονεῖτε, καὶ καταισχύνετε τοὺς μὴ ἔχοντας; τί εἴπω ὑμῖν; ἐπαινέσω ὑμᾶς; ἐν τούτῳ οὐκ ἐπαινῶ.

23 Ἐγὼ γὰρ παρέλαβον ἀπὸ τοῦ κυρίου, ὃ καὶ παρέδωκα ὑμῖν, ὅτι ὁ κύριος Ἰησοῦς ἐν τῇ νυκτὶ ᾗ παρεδίδετο ἔλαβεν ἄρτον 24 καὶ εὐχαριστήσας ἔκλασεν καὶ εἶπεν· Τοῦτό μού ἐστιν τὸ σῶμα τὸ ὑπὲρ ὑμῶν· τοῦτο ποιεῖτε εἰς τὴν ἐμὴν ἀνάμνησιν. 25 ὡσαύτως καὶ τὸ ποτήριον μετὰ τὸ δειπνῆσαι, λέγων· Τοῦτο τὸ ποτήριον ἡ καινὴ διαθήκη ἐστὶν ἐν τῷ ἐμῷ αἵματι· τοῦτο ποιεῖτε, ὁσάκις ἐὰν πίνητε, εἰς τὴν ἐμὴν ἀνάμνησιν. 26 ὁσάκις γὰρ ἐὰν ἐσθίητε τὸν ἄρτον τοῦτον καὶ τὸ ποτήριον πίνητε, τὸν θάνατον τοῦ κυρίου καταγγέλλετε, ἄχρι οὗ ἔλθῃ.

27 Ὥστε ὃς ἂν ἐσθίῃ τὸν ἄρτον ἢ πίνῃ τὸ ποτήριον τοῦ κυρίου ἀναξίως, ἔνοχος ἔσται τοῦ σώματος καὶ τοῦ αἵματος τοῦ κυρίου. 28 δοκιμαζέτω δὲ ἄνθρωπος ἑαυτόν, καὶ οὕτως ἐκ τοῦ ἄρτου ἐσθιέτω καὶ ἐκ τοῦ ποτηρίου πινέτω· 29 ὁ γὰρ ἐσθίων καὶ πίνων κρίμα ἑαυτῷ ἐσθίει καὶ πίνει μὴ διακρίνων τὸ σῶμα. 30 διὰ τοῦτο ἐν ὑμῖν πολλοὶ ἀσθενεῖς καὶ ἄρρωστοι καὶ κοιμῶνται ἱκανοί. 31 εἰ δὲ ἑαυτοὺς διεκρίνομεν, οὐκ ἂν ἐκρινόμεθα· 32 κρινόμενοι δὲ ὑπὸ κυρίου παιδευόμεθα, ἵνα μὴ σὺν τῷ κόσμῳ κατακριθῶμεν.

33 Ὥστε, ἀδελφοί μου, συνερχόμενοι εἰς τὸ φαγεῖν ἀλλήλους ἐκδέχεσθε. 34 εἴ τις πεινᾷ, ἐν οἴκῳ ἐσθιέτω, ἵνα μὴ εἰς κρίμα συνέρχησθε. Τὰ δὲ λοιπὰ ὡς ἂν ἔλθω διατάξομαι. (SBL Greek New Testament)

7 But in giving this instruction, I do not praise you, because you come together not for the better but for the worse. 18 For, in the first place, when you come together as a church, I hear that divisions exist among you; and in part I believe it. 19 For there must also be factions among you, so that those who are approved may become evident among you. 20 Therefore when you meet together, it is not to eat the Lord's Supper, 21 for in your eating each one takes his own supper first; and one is hungry and another is drunk. 22 What! Do you not have houses in which to eat and drink? Or do you despise the church of God and shame those who have nothing? What shall I say to you? Shall I praise you? In this I will not praise you.

23 For I received from the Lord that which I also delivered to you, that the Lord Jesus in the night in which He was betrayed took bread; 24 and when He had given thanks, He broke it and said, "This is My body, which is for you; do this in remembrance of Me." 25 In the same way He took the cup also after supper, saying, "This cup is the new covenant in My blood; do this, <u>as often as you drink it</u>, in remembrance of Me." 26 For <u>as often as you eat this bread and drink the cup, you proclaim the Lord's death until He comes.</u>

27 Therefore whoever eats the bread or drinks the cup of the Lord in an unworthy manner, shall be guilty of the body and the blood of the Lord. 28 But a man must examine himself, and in so doing he is to eat of the bread and drink of the cup. 29 For he who eats and drinks, eats and drinks judgment to himself if he does not judge the body rightly. 30 For this reason many among you are weak and sick, and a number sleep. 31 But if we judged ourselves rightly, we would not be judged. 32 But when we are judged, we are disciplined by the Lord so that we will not be condemned along with the world.

33 So then, my brethren, when you come together to eat, wait for one another. 34 If anyone is hungry, let him eat at home, so that you will not come together for judgment. The remaining matters I will arrange when I come. (ESV)

There are two key aspects of this text to answer the question. The first is frequency and the second is examination.

Frequency appears to be as often as the body gathered. We will need to get out of our twentieth century mindset of the meeting once a week. As was the custom of the Church in Acts, and since the church of the day was planted where there was a Jewish community first, we should see this frequency as daily. In that way, those who were some of the first in mass to accept the gospel, the poor, widow and needy could get their needs met at the table prepared for them both spiritually and physically.

The examination was equally important. The Didache in the next section will solidify this for the early church. It is important for us to know that profession, baptism, and examination are critically important to this celebration. It is a time to be thankful. To know Whom to thank, the Triune God, to know the reason for that thankfulness, the forgiveness of the cross and the life afforded through the resurrection of Jesus, and to then live in the Spirit of that thankfulness according to the will of God.

The witness of the Early Church:

Beginning with the book of Hebrews we look at the Lord's Supper as THE sacrifice of God for the sins of humanity. What Hebrews as a letter to God's people immersed in the Old Testament, does, is reflect the shadow of the Old Covenant that is cast on the work of God in the New Testament. Sacrifice was the center of Judaism. While the law is the vehicle, what that vehicle carries is sacrifice. Deuteronomy reflects that. The second book of the law reveals what we are to be and do socially and spiritually. The bottom line of it remains sacrifice culminated in Passover.

The Early Church's practice is difficult to sum up in a short section in a book that doesn't really deal with this specific topic. The Didache, an early catechism that dates from the later first century some seventy years after the death of Jesus to the early second century provides some insight into the Eucharistic practice if not frequency. In sections 9-10 we find the discussion of the Eucharist. While there are several fascinating things we could discuss, the only one that is pertinent to us is the one that opens the table ONLY to those who are baptized and have a relationship with Jesus Christ.

Ignatius wrote a bit later 70-107 A.D. says this in his letter to the Ephesians. "Try to gather together more frequently to celebrate God's Eucharist and to praise Him. For when you meet with frequency, Satan's powers are overthrown, and his destructiveness is undone by the unanimity of your faith. There is nothing better than peace by which all strife in heaven and earth is done away." Letter to Ephesians Section 13

This points to the urgency in and necessity of a frequent celebration of the supper as a family of God.

Polycarp, the bishop of Smyrna, c.70-155 A.D. in his notes entitled the Martyrdom of Polycarp, expresses the blessing he has been given to be martyred in the fashion of the cup of Christ pointing to the resurrection and the power of that resurrection shown through the immortality of the Holy Spirit manifested in the body. Section 14

In the First Apology of Justin (c.100-165 A.D.) says this about the Eucharist. "This food we call Eucharist, of which no one is allowed to partake except one who believes that the things we teach are true and has received the washing for forgiveness of sins for rebirth, and who lives as Christ handed down to us. For we do not receive these things as common bread or common drink; but as Jesus Christ our Savior being incarnate by God's word took flesh and blood for our salvation, so also we have been taught that the food consecrated by the word of prayer which comes from Him from which our flesh and blood are nourished by transformation is the flesh and blood of that incarnate Jesus."

There are other citations and theologians we could add. Suffice to say, the supper and celebration should 1) be done regularly and frequently, 2) be done as a family of God and community of believers 3) be done deliberately and with examination and confession 4) be done with the realization of the power of God's Word and Spirit to effect transformation in the life of the believer.

It is for this reason this book has been written

❖ What are the biggest mistakes you've made or seen regarding communion practices?

The biggest mistakes I have seen would all fall under a couple of umbrella headings; misunderstanding the significance of the supper for people and diminishing the meaning of the supper for others. For example, under the first heading, considering the sacrament to be a mere memorial is I believe biblically and theologically a huge mistake. What we are essentially saying is that the Lord's Supper is a mere symbol without any transformative power in the believer's life. In addition to that it does nothing to enhance my relationship with the God who has given me this meal. There are other mistakes that would fall under the parameters of this error.

The second, we discussed a bit earlier. To come to the table with less than the seriousness of what it is we celebrate and what we expect to happen from it is a huge mistake.

Bibliography

This is a truncated Bibliography. I am including the books that were the most helpful in not only forming a sense of what the Lord's Supper has been and ought to be, but also helped immensely in developing an understanding of the frequency of communion and the variety of themes that are present within it. It is an eclectic list. I hope it is helpful to you.

Communion Theology

Calvin, John, Treatises on the Sacraments: Tracts by John Calvin, Christian Heritage Publishers, Reformation Heritage Books, Grand Rapids, Mi., 2002

Crockett, William R., Eucharist: Symbol of Transformation,Pueblo Publishing Co., New York, New York,1989.

De Arteaga, William L., Forgotten Power: The Significance of the Lord's Supper in Revival, Zondervan Publishing, Grand Rapids, Mi., 2002

De Silva, David A., Sacramental Life: Spiritual Formation Through the Book of Common Prayer, InterVarsity Press, Downers Grove Ill., 2008.

Fredman, Ruth Gruber, The Passover Seder: Afikoman in Exile, University of Pennsylvania Press, Philadelphia, 1981.

Jeremias, Joachim, The Eucharistic Words of Jesus, SCM Press Limited, London, 1966.

La Verdiere, Eugene, The Eucharist in the New Testament and the Early Church, Liturgical Press, Collegeville, Minn., 1996.

Mathison, Keith A., Given For You: Reclaiming Calvin's Doctrine of the Lord's Supper, P & R Publishing Co. Phillipsburg, New Jersey, 2002.

Moore - Keish, Martha L., Do This in Remembrance of Me: A Ritual Approach to Reformed Eucharistic Theology, Wm. B. Eerdmans Co., Grand Rapids, Mi., 2008.

Nowen, Henri J.M., With Burning Hearts: A Mediation on the Eucharistic Life, Orbis Press, Maryknoll, New York, 1994.

Rordorf, Willy, et.al., The Eucharist of the Early Christians, The Liturgical Press, Collegeville, Minnesota, 1978.

Owen, John, Communion with God, Christian Focus Publications, Scotland, 2007.

Oxenden, Ashton, The Earnest Communicant, Reformation Heritage Books and Free Reformed Publications, 2009.

Payne, Leanne, Real Presence: The Christian Worldview of C.S. Lewis as Incarnational Reality, Baker Books, Grand Rapids, Mi., 1995.

Rosen, Ceil and Moishe, Christ in the Passover: Why is this night different, Moody Bible Institute, Chicago, Ill., 1978.

Schmemann, Alexander, The Eucharist, St. Vladimir's Seminary Press, Crestwood, New York, 1987.

Schmidt, Dan, Taken By Communion: How the Lord's Supper Nourishes the Soul, Baker Books, Grand Rapids, Mi.,2003.

Stookey, Laurence Hull, Eucharist: Christ's Feast with the Church, Abingdon Press, Nashville, Tenn., 1993.

Thurian, Max, The Mystery of the Eucharist, Wm. B. Eerdmans, Grand Rapids, Mi., 1981.

Warren, Meredith C.J., My Flesh Is Meat Indeed: A Non-Sacramental Reading of John 6:51-58, Fortress Press, Minneapolis, Mi., 2015.

Welker, Michael, What Happens in Holy Communion?, Wm. B. Eerdmans Publishing, Grand Rapids, Mi., 2000.

Witherington III, Ben, Making a Meal of It: Rethinking the Theology of the Lord's Supper, Baylor University Press, Waco Texas, 2007.

The list of books included here on prayer are not by any stretch an exhaustive list of books on prayer. These are the ones that I have relied upon in the past and in the material of the liturgies that you find included here. There are many others that I have used sparsely.

Prayers

Brueggemann, Walter, Awed to Heaven, Rooted in Earth, Augsburg Press, Minneapolis, Minn., 2003.

Gillis, Martha S., ed., Let Us Pray: Reformed Prayers for Christian Worship, Geneva Press, Louisville, Kentucky, 2002.

Kirk, James G., When We Gather: A Book of Prayers for Worship, Geneva Press, Louisville, Kentucky, 2001.

Old, Hughes Oliphant, Leading in Prayer: A Workbook for Worship, Wm. B. Eerdmans Publishing, Grand Rapids, Mi., 1995.

Rice, Howard L., & Lamar Williamson Jr., ed., A Book of Reformed Prayers, Westminster John Knox Press, Louisville, Kentucky, 1998.

The section on music below is merely representative of the resources I have availed myself of when working on putting worship services together with a theme for communion. Your list will most certainly include others.

Music

The Celebration Hymnal: Songs and Hymns for Worship, Word Music/Integrity Music, Word/Integrity,1997.

Cherry, Constance, The Contemporary Psalter: Bringing the Ancient to Life, CMC Unlimited, 2000.

Cherry, Constance, Proclaim New Hope, Hope Publishing Co. Carol Stream, Ill., 2001

Lift Up Your Hearts: Psalms, Hymns and Spiritual Songs, Faith Alive Publishing, Grand Rapids, Mi.,2013.

Psalter Hymnal, CRC Publications, Grand Rapids, Mi.,1987.

Renew: Songs & Hymns for Blended Worship, Hope Publishing Co., Carol Stream, Ill., 1995.

Service Book and Hymnal (of the Lutheran Church), Augsburg Publishing House, Minneapolis, Minn., 1958.

Trinity Psalter Hymnal, Trinity Psalter Hymnal Joint Venture Committee, Willow Grove, Pa., 2018.

Worship Hymnal, Cloverdale United Reformed Church, 2020.
The resources given below are only a small sampling of what is out there for you to use for setting up liturgy for the service of the table.

Liturgical Forms

Bartels, Ernest, Take Eat, Take Drink: The Lord's Supper through the Centuries, Concordia Publishing House, St. Louis, Mo., 2004.

Farwell, James, This Is the Night: Suffering, Salvation, and the Liturgies of Holy Week, T & T Clark, New Yok, London, 2005.

Henry, Jim, In Remembrance of Me: A Manual on Observing the Lord's Supper, Broadman and Holman Publishers, Nashville, Tennessee, 1998.

Parks, Marty, Come to the Table: A Resource Book for Holy Communion, Lillenas Publishing Co., Kansas City, Mo., 2002.

Printed in the United States
by Baker & Taylor Publisher Services